The Advanced Stock Market and Day Trading Guide

Learn How You Can Day Trade and Start Investing in Stocks for a Living, Follow Beginners Strategies for Trading Penny Stocks, Bonds, Options, and Forex.

By Neil Sharp

"The Advanced Stock Market and Day Trading Guide: Learn How You Can Day Trade and Start Investing in Stocks for a Living, Follow Beginners Strategies for Trading Penny Stocks, Bonds, Options, and Forex." Written by "Neil Sharp".

The Advanced Stock Market and Day Trading Guide is a bundle of the books "The Advanced Stock Market Investing Guide", & "The Advanced Day Trading Guide".

Hope You Enjoy!

The Advanced Stock Market Investing Guide

Follow This Step by Step Beginners Trading Guide for Learning How to Trade Penny Stocks, Bonds, Options, Forex, and Shares; to Become a Stock Trader Today!

By Neil Sharp

Table of Contents

Table of Contents
Introduction
Chapter 1: The Importance of Investing
Chapter 2: Stock Market Fundamentals

    Definition of financial markets
    Equities
    Bonds
    Categories of bonds
    Options Trading
    FOREX
    Performance indicators
    Impact on the average investor

Chapter 3: Investment Vehicles

    Certificates of Deposit
    Mutual Funds
    Annuities
    Portfolios

Chapter 4: Day Trading

    How to become an investor
    How to purchase funds online
    How to purchase a tracker fund
    Investment platforms
    How to determine when to buy
    How to determine when to sell

Chapter 5: The Language of Investing

    The importance of diversification
    Annual return on investments
    Risk Management

Chapter 6: Starting from Scratch: How to Grow Like the Pros

Warren Buffet
Chris Gardner
Ken Langone
Oprah Winfrey
Andrew Carnegie

Chapter 7: Governance

Legislation governing brokers
Legislation applicable to investors
Tax considerations

Chapter 8: How to Win the Stock Market Game

Value investing
Growth investing
Income investing
Passive investing

Chapter 9: Advanced Trading Strategies

Short selling
Buying on margin
Portfolio Management

Conclusion
Table of Contents
Introduction
Chapter 1: The fundamentals of day trading

Characteristics of a day trader

Characteristic #1: Discipline
Characteristic #2: Patience
Characteristic #3: Flexibility
Characteristic #4: Resiliency
Characteristic #5: Independence
Characteristic #6: Vision

Day trading as a full-time career

- **The day trading differs from other types of trading**
- **Benefits of day trading**
- **Drawbacks of day trading**
- **Basics of day trading futures**
- **Day trading FOREX**
- **Day trading options**
- **Day trading equities**

Chapter 2: Trading basics

- Bid and Ask
- Types of Orders

Chapter 3: Setting up a brokerage account

- Overview
- Fees
- Account Minimums
- Requirements
- Cash or margin
- How to open an account
- Advantages of brokerage accounts
- What to watch out for

Chapter 4: How to choose the right stocks

- Company revenue
- Earnings per share
- Return on Equity
- Assets (-) liabilities = equity
- Analyst recommendations
- Positive earnings
- Earnings forecast
- Earnings growth
- PEG Ratio
- Industry price earnings

Days to cover

Chapter 5: The best time to trade

Overview
Market opening
Market closing
Avoiding pitfalls

Chapter 6: Reducing risk in day trading

Determining the right amount of investable capital
Setting up a stop-loss point
Working with a broker
Taking breaks when needed
Keeping emotions in check
Avoiding fads

Chapter 7: Day trading strategies

Candlestick charting
Bullish candlesticks
Bearish candlesticks
The ABCD pattern
Reverse trading
Moving average trend trading
Resistance trading
Opening range breakout
Red to green trading
Data analysis in trading
Technical analysis in day trading
The bottom line

Chapter 8: Advanced trading strategies

Gap up, inside Bar, breakout strategy
Gap up, attempt to fill, breakout
The gap up, afternoon breakout
Fibonacci retracement pattern

Gap down, fill down, inside bar, breakout

Chapter 9: Tips for completing a successful trade

Building up a watch list
Deciding on the right stocks for you
Putting an entry and exit strategy into place
Purchasing desired stocks
Paying attention to the market until the trade is completed
Selling stocks when reaching original exit points
Reflecting on trades and extracting lessons learned
Researching information for future trades
Automating trade processes

Conclusion

Introduction

Congratulations on purchasing "***The Advanced Stock Market Investing Guide*** : *Follow This Step by Step Beginners Trading Guide for Learning How to Trade Penny Stocks, Bonds, Options, Forex, and Shares; to Become a Stock Trader Today!*" Great care was taken in ensuring that the information contained herein is not only useful but relevant.

The following pages contain a trove of actionable information and advice which the average individual can put into practice in order to become a stock trader. Since this is a rather extensive topic, the contents of each chapter have been boiled down to their essence. This means that there is no fluff; just the good stuff.

Also, great care has been taken to ensure that the concepts described throughout this book are explained in a clear, plain language that is devoid of complicated business jargon. As such, this book isn't about sounding smart – it's about actually being smart!

I am sure that you have chosen this book because you are interested in finding out how you can make more money than you are today. And there is nothing wrong with that! In fact, I commend your desire to earn a better living and provide a higher quality of life for your loved ones.

The main objective of this book is to provide you with a guide filled with relevant information that will allow you to become a stock trader and actually make money.

If you are looking for practice examples of how financial markets work, then you have come to the right place.

Each chapter covers one fundamental area of stock trading.

First, we will take a close look at the importance of investing and how you can make money in financial markets by choosing your investments wisely.

Then, we will have an in-depth discussion of the different investment vehicles available to you. This means that you will learn about how these investments work, the pitfalls that come with them, and how you can make money.

Next, we will look into day trading. This is a key chapter since it will enable you to get a good sense of what it takes to become a stock trader. Through analysis and insight, you will be able to make up your mind and decide if day trading is for you.

If you feel that day trading isn't your thing, there are also two chapters based on investment strategies that you can implement without actually getting your hands dirty. These strategies are meant to put your money to work without taking up too much of your time.

Also, we will discuss how legislation and taxes can play a role in your investment strategy. In particular, we will have an in-depth discussion on how reckless investment practices led to the financial crisis of 2008.

Finally, we will go over the lives of some of the most famous investor in history. The stories of these individuals are meant to inspire you, but also provide you with role models that you can emulate. These are not flamboyant traders like those seen in Hollywood movies. These are ordinary folks that made it big through hard work and savvy investment.

So, what are you waiting for?

Let's jump right in and learn how to become a stock trader today!

Chapter 1: The Importance of Investing

"Money doesn't grow on trees."

Have you ever heard that expression? I'm sure you have.

And, it's true.

Nevertheless, money does grow, just in a different sense.

Most folks obtain money through their jobs. When a person gets a job, they are compensated for the work they do. Whatever the work that is done, the person receives a sum of money in exchange.

That money is then used to acquire the goods and services needed in order to live. Some folks manage to save some of their earnings at the end of the month, some break even, and some are in a hole.

This cycle of working for money ties the earnings of an individual to their work. So, the more they work, the more they earn at least in theory.

Some folks choose to go through life working, paying their taxes and perhaps collecting a pension at the end of their career.

Other folks choose to blow all their money and end up poor at the end of their productive lives.

Other folks choose to invest part of their money.

In economic terms, investing is the result of saving. When a person saves money, that surplus amount of money is eligible for investment since the person doesn't actually need to spend. If they did, then they wouldn't have saved it.

Unless an individual chooses to dig a hole in the ground and bury their savings, money tends to find its way to investors.

One simple example of this is leaving money in the bank.

The money that is deposited into a bank account will make its way to investors through what is called "fractional reserve lending."

This concept indicates that the money that is deposited by customers into a bank is eligible to be loaned out to other customers. So, when a customer comes to the bank and asks for a loan, the bank can loan out the money deposited by the other customers.

By law, banks are required to keep a fraction of that money in the vault for customers who want to make a withdrawal. Hence, fractional reserve lending means that banks must keep a small part of their customers' deposits and may loan out the rest.

This is a simple example of how savings translate into investment.

On the whole, investment is needed to drive a country's economy. Under a capitalist system, the more money circulates, the more good and services change hands. In addition, the more money that ends up in people's pockets.

That's why burying your savings in the backyard will kill any economic momentum.

As an individual, investing represents an opportunity to make money grow literally.

The most commonly known type of investment is a bank account.

Bank accounts will pay an amount of money called "interest" calculated on how much money a customer has deposited in that bank.

Other common types of investments are 401(k)'s or even businesses. These investments use money to make more money.

A 401(k) is essentially a bank account in which an employee contributes money to it every month. The financial institution that secures the 401(k) will take that money and invest it in other ventures. The money that financial institution makes is what is used to pay off the interest accrued by that 401(k).

If an individual chooses to invest in a business, the profits earned from that business will also make money grow.

Over time, money invested may generate enough income to a point where it can fund a person's lifestyle. This is the main purpose of saving up for retirement. You may also hear about those individuals who have "retired early."

In essence, retiring means that you no longer have to work in order to finance your lifestyle. And this can be done through investing.

Now, that takes us into what is known as the stock market.

The stock market, or financial markets for that matter, enable individual investors to take their money and put it to work. The series of financial instruments and vehicles available to investors allows them to earn money from placing their surplus earnings in the hands of individuals who will make use of that money.

By investing in the stock market, investors are not looking to pursue business opportunities that imply the production of goods and services. These are speculative activities that are based on "paper assets." In other words, there are no tangible objects at play. Rather, the investments made are in buying and selling assets which will produce a yield.

This yield is basically the profits made on investments in financial markets.

For those individuals who seek to secure their future, grow their net worth or achieve the lifestyle they have always dreamed about, then investing in financial markets is a plausible way of achieving this.

However, investing in financial markets is no easy task for those who don't know what they are doing. For those who do, they are able to navigate the waters of the system and use it to their advantage.

Of course, becoming an expert at trading in financial markets takes some time and training. But with the right coaching and information, becoming an expert is a lot easier than you might think. The important thing is to have the willingness to put in the time and effort it takes to learn.

The benefits of investing outweigh the risks by far as long as you know what you are doing. This is why investing in the stock market is not recommended for individuals who do not have the know-how and are not willing to seek qualified financial advice.

But by reading this guide, you will be able to take your own investment strategy and maximize your chances at making it.

Will you be the next Wall Street millionaire?
Maybe!

And I use the word "maybe" because it's up to you to make the right choices based on accurate information, a strong "gut" and common sense.

In the next chapter, we will take a closer look at how financial markets work.

Chapter 2: Stock Market Fundamentals

The words "stock market" are two of the most magical words in the English language.

To some, the stock market has been a source of great wealth and opportunity. To others, these words have meant headaches and stress.

The fact of the matter is that much of the stress and anxiety that comes from investing in the stock market comes from a lack of understanding into its nature. Often, you will hear much information and advice regarding the stocks and other financial assets. However, the so-called experts and pundits on television do little to actually explain the fundamentals of investing.

Investing in financial markets does not have to become stressful, even if it may be painful at times. With the right understanding of how financial markets work, you can begin to invest wisely and successfully. That is why it is necessary to lay some groundwork.

In this chapter, we will cover the basics and fundamentals of financial markets. We will take a deep look into definitions of the most important concepts pertaining to investing in financial markets. Moreover, the information contained herein should be considered as a guide, a road map if you will, on how to navigate through the various investment vehicles and instruments available to the average investor.

It is important to note that this chapter is not so much about providing financial advice on what the best investment vehicles are, but rather, it is about having a holistic approach on the various types of financial assets at the disposal of the average investor.

Also, it is worth noting that the term "average investor" refers to a regular individual who is looking to put some of the hard-earned cash into equities, bonds or any other assets. We are not considering the large, institutional investors, such as investment banks of hedge funds, as they play under different rules and circumstances.

As such, the average investor is someone who is looking to take advantage of the opportunities the market affords and multiply their savings into a greater amount that can serve as income down the road. Furthermore, large, institutional investors dabble in derivates markets. This is something that we will refer to throughout this book, but we will not be touching upon in too much detail as we are focused on getting you off the ground.

So, buckle up. This chapter is filled with concepts, definitions, and above all, actionable information which will surely open your eyes into the realm of possibilities available in the stock market. Most importantly, you will be able to form your own, informed opinion about what is available to you as an average investor. That way, you can begin planning your investment strategy right off the bat!

Definition of financial markets

The stock market, or equities market, is one of several different markets that make up a greater sum known as "financial markets."

In essence, financial markets are a place (either physical or virtual) where lenders, investors, borrowers, and buyers come together to buy and sell equities, securities, derivatives, commodities, bonds or financial assets such as mutual funds or exchange-traded funds (ETFs).

Let's take a closer look at each item:

- **Equities**: These are shares of publicly traded companies that are available on major indices such as the Dow Jones, Nasdaq and the S&P 500 in the United States. There are also other major financial markets throughout the world in countries such as Japan, Germany, Spain, and the UK.

- **Securities**: The are debt instruments which lenders can package and sell to investors. For example, banks can package mortgages and sell them to hedge funds who get a return on their investment from the interest paid by borrowers.
- **Derivative**: These are complex financial instruments mainly available to institutional investors. Derivates, as its name suggests, are instruments which are "derived" from an underlying asset. These instruments are often high-risk and may represent a high-risk, high reward proposition for investors.
- **Commodities**: These are investments into physical goods such as oil, agricultural products, precious metals or any other physical good produced by companies.
- **Mutual funds**: This is a pool of money collected by a financial institution from investors which is then used to buy and sell a portfolio of financial assets. The return on the entire portfolio of investors is then distributed among the total pool of investors.
- **Exchange Traded Funds**: These funds are similar to mutual funds with the difference that there is an underlying asset to the fund. For instance, oil can be traded by way of an ETF. An investor can

buy into an oil ETF and collect a return from the profits in oil prices.

- **Bonds**: These are debt instruments issued by sovereign governments or private corporations. The bond market is the biggest financial market in the world. Some countries, like the United States, allow private citizens to purchase government bonds while other countries sell them on international financial markets only to institutional investors.

The financial instruments mentioned above are called "paper assets" as they represent investments of cash into vehicles which are not physically tangible. Except for commodities, financial assets are essentially represented by certificates which are proof of ownership. Moreover, many of these investments are not represented by cold, hard cash, but rather, are represented by money in digital form.

ETFs for commodities such as oil, precious metals (gold and silver), industrial metals (copper, tin, aluminum), agricultural products (sugar, coffee, corn, cattle), or energy products (coal, natural gas) may or may not come along with a physical allocation. What that means is that if the ETF contract does not specify that the investor will take physical delivery of the commodity, then the investor will only receive a monetary payment corresponding to the investment made.

Conversely, when an ETF contract does specify a physical allocation, the investor may choose to take physical delivery of the commodity specified in the contract. So, the investor can cash out by receiving sacks of coffee instead of a check for the monetary amount indicated in the contract.

Now, let's move on to a more in-depth definition of each financial instrument.

Equities

Equities are the most-commonly known financial assets.

This is what is commonly referred to as the "stock market."

In essence, stocks are "shares" of a company which any investor can purchase. Each share is a proportion of ownership of that specific company. For example, if a company issues 1000 shares, then 50% ownership of that company would represent ownership of 500 shares. By the same token, one share represents ownership of that company, albeit in a minuscule proportion.

When a company is formed, corporate law requires it to be "incorporated." This means that the company must become a formal legal entity. This means that a regular "mom and pop" business does not qualify as it is most likely a sole proprietorship. Hence, small businesses do not fall into this category.

One thing about small business though: hedge funds invest in what is called "private equities." That means that they buy into companies which are not publicly traded. Think of "Shark Tank" when considering private equities. These are entrepreneurs or startup companies that have a significant value proposition which investors want to get into at its early stages so they can clean up when the company grows.

So, when a company reaches a point when they are large enough to draw considerable interest from larger, institutional investments such as hedge funds and investment banks (also sovereign wealth funds may throw their hat in the ring), the company will enter a process called its "initial public offering" or IPO.

In the IPO process, all of the owners of the company, which is still private, decide they will put their shares for sale to anyone who chooses to purchase them. The valuation of those shares depends on the company's profit outlook.

For instance, if ABC Company decides to "go public," the company must be valued. The actual book value of the company is irrelevant as investors are paying for the dividends they will earn per share. So, if the company is highly profitable, then the shareholders, at the time of the IPO, will have an asking price for their shares.

Let's say that the asking price is $100 per share. This asking price is tested in the market to gauge interest at that price point. If the company is red-hot, investors may signal, by word of mouth, if they are willing to pay that much, or even more. Also, investors may feel the valuation is too high, and they would be willing to pay less.

Next, an authorized broker, usually a large investment bank such as Merrill Lynch or JP Morgan in the United States, will "underwrite" the IPO. In other words, they will present ABC Company's shares to the market. This is like having a middleman sell the shares of the company to investors.

Derivatives come into play here, since IPO underwriters must have another financial institution insure the IPO. The insurance needs to be included in case something goes wrong and the deal falls through. For example, fraudulent activity is discovered, or an event of significant impact disrupts the company's operations. As such, insurance protects investors' money going into the deal.

The entire IPO process is supervised by the Securities and Exchange Commission (SEC) in the United States in order to ensure that the entire process has been done according to regulations. Every country that has financial markets will have their own regulatory agency.

Once the IPO is ready, the company will enter one of the financial markets available in the world. Not all companies are traded in the United States. American companies may choose to be traded on international markets such as in London or Hong Kong. Companies from outside the United States may choose to be included in American stock exchanges.

Once the IPO has gone public, then the shares are up for sale. This is when brokerage firms and other investment institutions can choose to scoop up the shares. This is where the early investors clean up.

Let's assume that XYZ capital funded ABC Company and provided them with seed capital at its outset. They invested $10,000 in exchange for 100 shares. That works out to $100 a share. The IPO valuation of ABC Company was listed at $1,000 a share. When ABC Company went public, XYZ capital received $1000 per share when it originally paid $100.

This example is not uncommon but not frequent.

The average investor will jump into the race well after the IPO.

While shares of all publicly traded companies are technically available to anyone with the cash to invest, they are not always up for sale.

For instance, if XYZ Capital holds 100 shares of Apple, they may choose to simply sit on them and not sell. Perhaps they are waiting for the price to go up and then turn around and sell them. Or, the company has not posted strong earnings and XYZ Capital is waiting for Apple to rebound before deciding to sell.

This brings up to the next point: the price of shares on the open market is set by supply and demand.

In economic terms, demand is driven by the amount of money available to invest. This money comes from two main sources: the average investor, that is, mon and pop who have some extra money set aside and would like to put it to work, and institutional investors.

Institutional investors are hedge funds, investment banks or even sovereign wealth fund.

A hedge fund is a "club" of wealthy individuals who pool their money together. The hedge fund itself is a financial institution which is in charge of managing the money to the benefit of its members. Needless to say, hedge funds are thirsty for profits and will always demand higher yields, and higher returns. In addition, hedge funds tend to be cowboys, that is, they will take on the highest amount of risk, if and when, they pay off is commensurate to the risk.

Investment banks are more traditional financial institutions such as Merrill Lynch, or JP Morgan in the United States, or huge international banks such as HSBC, Scotiabank, Deutsche Bank, Credit Suisse to name a few. These aren't necessarily banks in the traditional sense of the word, that is, a savings and loan bank, but rather, these are formal wealth management companies that are governed by the prevailing financial regulations of the country in which they are incorporated.

Unlike investment banks, hedge funds often do not fall under the same regulatory umbrella. This is why they engage in higher-risk activities since many countries, especially in Europe, consider hedge funds to be private enterprises. Therefore, they are no different than a hardware store. The only difference is that they don't sell hammers. Instead, they sell financial assets.

Lastly, sovereign wealth funds are institutions which are represented by countries. These funds are generally state-owned institutions that have the official backing of a sovereign state. For example, the largest sovereign wealth fund in the world is China. Consequently, this is official Chinese state money which can be invested in equities, commodities and other financial vehicles. Not all countries have these funds, and most sovereign funds are not closely regulated by their country of origin.

The investment money available in a country, region or the entire world, will compete for the best investments. This competition is what drives up the price of the best investments available. This is why bonds are the largest financial market since they offer lower risk and almost guaranteed returns. The only way a bond cannot be repaid is if a country defaults on its debt such as the case of Argentina or Russia.

When available investment money enters the market, the best investments get snatched up first. But since other investors are looking to put their money to work, they might be willing to pay more for those very same investments. This is what drives up the price of a bond, stock, or even commodity.

Also, if a company falls flat and their earnings do not live up to investors' expectations, shareholders may choose to dump their shares in that company. That drives the price down as buyers may not be willing to pay the same amount of money for those shares. That may mean that current shareholders may take a loss or just a lesser profit.

Let's consider ABC Company. ABC Company's shares went up to $1000 per share after its IPO. It's a hot tech stock, and everybody wants in. The initial investors cleaned up they made a nice bit of change on the IPO.

It has come time for ABC Company to report its quarterly earnings. In their report, ABC Company reported higher-than-expected profits. This sends the stock soaring as everyone wants a piece of the action. The stock goes from $1000 to $1100 in a matter of minutes. In this case, demand from investors dries up the price as not all shareholders decide to sell. They want to hold on to the stock because it's doing so well. So, those who do decide to sell make a greater profit because there is a limited number of shares available. And, investors are going wild.

On the contrary, let's assume that ABC Company's earnings were lower than expected. This means that shareholders are now worried about what might happen to the company. They might choose to hold, hoping that it will rebound in the next quarter.

Other shareholders might think that the company is in trouble and decide they want to get out. They bought into ABC Company at $1000 a share. But because its earnings were lower than expected, buyers may choose to pay $900 a share. They figure they will buy low hoping that the company will rebound and make a profit in the next quarter. Those shareholders who bought at $1000 and sell at $900, have now taken a $100 per share hit.

As you can see, the forces of supply and demand are what drive the price of equities. Therefore, companies need to be careful they don't issue too many shares or else the price of each share will drop. Conversely, some companies engage in what is called "buybacks." This is when a company buys back its own stock. Since there is less of the stock available, the price will go up as investors will try to find more shares but will have to pay more for the existing ones.

Another item to consider is the definition of a stock exchange.

As mentioned earlier, there are many stock exchanges throughout the world. They belong to specific countries and are governed by the legislation of their home country.

In the United States, there are several stock exchanges.

- New York Stock Exchange (Wall Street)
- Chicago Stock Exchange

- Boston Stock Exchange
- Miami Stock Exchange
- Philadelphia Stock Exchange

Each one of these exchanges is a physical location where traders meet to buy and sell equities, commodities or other securities.

Most people often confuse stock exchanges with indices such as the Dow Jones and the Nasdaq. The difference is that the Dow and Nasdaq are not physical locations where traders meet to do business. They are merely statistical measures of one portion of the market.

For example, the Dow Jones measures the top 30 companies in the market. This measure tracks their performance and determines the trend for the market. The Nasdaq was the first computerized trading system that eventually became a stock market index. It generally tracks "tech" companies though it is not exclusive to this sector. Another index is the S&P 500 which is a measure of the top 500 companies which are not included in the Dow Jones.

At this point, it is important to take a look at the other financial assets available to investors.

Bonds

The bond market is perhaps the most important market in the world.

Bonds are certificates of debt which sovereign nations or private corporations issue. These instruments allow institutions to obtain funding on the promise that they will pay that money back, plus interest when the bond matures, that is, when the time is up.

There are several terms on bonds. They range from 30 days to 30 years. They come in all shapes and sizes since they respond to the needs of the institutions issuing them.

The interest that bonds pay out to buyers is called "yield." The issuer basically sets the yield, though it varies depending on market forces. The yield itself does not change. That is the interest that is paid on it. For example, if a bond has a $100 face value, a coupon of 10%, then the 10% would be considered the yield. Note that the coupon is calculated on the face value of the bond.

If the issuing county of that bond is a stable and solid state, then investors may choose to pay more than the $100 face value in order to purchase a safe asset. Let's assume that investors are willing to pay $110 for the $100 bond. Then considering the 10% coupon, that is, $10 worth of interest, then the yield would be calculated as 10/110 = 0.09 or 9%. This means the yield has fallen to 9%. The logic is that the safer the investment, the lower the yield.

On the other hand, this issuing country is having economic troubles and may not live up to their financial obligations. In other words, they are at risk of defaulting or not paying back their bonds. So, bondholders may choose to drop the bond like a hot potato. Bondholders will short, or sell for less, and take $90 on the $100 face value bond. This means that the yield has risen since the coupon is still 10%, but the price paid for the bond is less. Here is the calculation: 10/90 = 0.111 or 11.1%. The yield is now 11% because market logic dictates that the higher the risk, the higher the yield.

Sovereign governments may choose to place their bonds in the United States stock exchanges, or in any other stock exchange, they consider appropriate. And like equities or stocks, bonds must be underwritten by a reputable financial institution if they are placed in the United States. In other countries, the laws of that country govern the placement of bonds.

Bonds may also be insured. This insurance of bonds falls into the derivatives market as insurers are essentially betting that a country will or will not default on its debt obligations. If the country does default, then insurers will have to pay out the policies of their insured. If the country does not default, then insurers only collect the premiums paid by their clients for the right to have their bonds insured.

One other important aspect of bonds is that they may be issued in any currency. This is very important since currencies tend to fluctuate, that is, gain or lose value. If a country issues bonds, and that country's currency tanks, or loses significant value, then investors may just decide to dump the bonds for whatever they can get. This can cause a country to enter an economic meltdown.

Therefore, both countries and private corporations may choose to issue their bonds in currencies other than that of their home country. So, countries and corporations may choose to issue their bonds in US Dollars, Euros, Swiss Francs, or perhaps Yen. The important thing is that the currency is stable and accepted by investors around the world. If a bond is issued in a currency that is not trusted by investors, the bond would essentially be worthless.

Corporate bonds function the same way as sovereign bonds. These bonds are a means for companies to obtain financing through other means that isn't through the issuance of stock. Corporate bonds are underwritten by reputable financial intermediaries and are insured in the derivatives market. And just like sovereign bonds, the higher the risk, the higher the yield.

Categories of bonds

There are several different categories of bonds. That is, not all bonds are created equal.

In the previous section, we discussed two types of bonds: sovereign bonds and corporate bonds. They both function in the same manner and their yield is treated in the same way.

Now, let's have a closer look at the types of bonds out there:

• **Sovereign bonds**: As indicated in the previous section, there are bonds which are issued by sovereign nations. In the United States, they are called Treasury Bills or T-Bills. They are issued by the US Treasury and are bought by the intermediary banks through the Federal Reserve System. Most nations issue their bonds through their central banks.

• **Non-Sovereign bonds**: These types of bonds are usually issued for special purposes such as war bonds. They are a temporary means of raising capital and are usually linked to a very specific event such as a war. Countries may also issue these bonds to pay for expensive public works or to fund their currency.

- **High-quality corporate bonds:** We have already discussed corporate bonds. Yet, there are two types of corporate bonds — high and low quality. High-quality bonds are determined by a company's credit rating. This is done through a ratings agency such as Fitch, Standard and Poor's or Moody's. These are solid companies with great track records, healthy finances and low risk of default. They have a lower yield since they have a lower risk.

- **Low-quality bonds**: These are the so-called "junk bonds." These are bonds that are issued by corporations with not-so-good track records and may even represent a risk of default. These corporations offer little in the way of interest, but if they do pay up, the yield may become very attractive. This is an example of a high-risk, high-reward situation. Junk bonds are excessively risk and if several firms default at the same time, may cause massive losses in the bond market.

- **Municipal bonds**: Local governments issue these. In the United States, individual states and cities may issues bonds. This is not always possible in other countries. So, it's up to each country's individual governance.

- **Mortgage-backed bonds**: These types of bonds are actively traded in the derivatives market. These bonds consist in mortgage lenders issuing bonds in order to obtain funding for the sole purpose of lending money to homebuyers in order to finance the purchase of their homes. In essence, these bonds are what funds home purchases. When they are sold, other institutions become the owners of the mortgages that are attached to those bonds. These are some of the most-favored investments by hedge funds.
- **Debt-collateralized bonds**: These are high-risk bonds as they are issued by lenders who are looking to fund the issuance of credit to customers. These credits could come in the way of loans, credit cards or car loans. These loans have a high-risk of default but do offer the best returns to investors.

Options Trading

Options trading is part of the derivatives market. An option, as its name suggests, gives a person the option to buy, or sell, shares, but does not create an obligation. It is a derivative since it is valued on an underlying asset, in this case, stock.

Options are issued when there is speculation about a stock price. Essentially, the shareholder may choose to sell at a given price as specified in the contract but is not ultimately obligated to do so. The same goes for a buyer. What an option does is lock in a buy/sell price on that asset.

There are two parts to an options contract: the "put" and "call." A put option consists in granting someone the right to sell the underlying asset. When that happens, the parties involved in the contract agree on the price and terms of the sale.

A call option grants someone the right to buy the underlying asset in question. By this logic, if the buyer chooses to purchase the asset, the buyer will do so at the price and terms indicated in the contract.

The advantage of options is that it enables parties to agree on price and terms before actually engaging in the deal. Trades done outside options are subject to market forces. Therefore, buyers and seller may end up losing out on good deals.

Furthermore, options may lock in a price, similar to a futures contract, though a futures contract is tied to a commodity, such as oil, as the underlying asset whereas options have equities or even bonds, as the underlying asset.

FOREX

Foreign Exchange (FOREX) is a highly speculative market in which two, or more currencies, are pitted against each other. This market consists of buying and selling currencies based on their market value. It is a highly liquid market since investors are dealing specifically in money.

Equity or bond markets are not a liquid as FOREX since investors own paper assets which may, or may not, have enough funding to back their trades. This may result in a margin call thus leaving investors' positions unprotected. The end result could be an investor defaulting and needing to dump equities or securities in the market, at any price, in order to obtain cash.

As such, FOREX enables investors to trade in highly liquid assets denominated in currencies. There are FOREX ETFs which are essentially guaranteed to pay out since the underlying asset is cold, hard cash. Investors cannot enter the FOREX market unless they have the actual cash to do so.

FOREX looks at the exchange rates between two currencies. In essence, these could be two currencies of any two countries in the world. So, the combinations are virtually endless. It is also highly speculative because investors are betting against an appreciation or depreciation of one currency versus another.

For example, a trader buys 10,000 Euros at an exchange rate of 1EUR:1.18USD. That means that the investor would need 11,800 USD in order to purchase the 10,000 EUR. If the exchange rate changes from 1EUR:1.18USD to 1EUR:1.25USD, then the trader now has 12,500USD. He has made a profit of $700.

Performance indicators

Like anything in life, financial markets have indicators. These indicators may vary for international markets. But for the US markets, there are several indicators which investors can track in order to determine market trends.

We have already mentioned the Dow Jones, Nasdaq and S&P 500. These indices serve as an initial evaluation of stock market performance.

When the markets are doing well, they are said to be a "bull market." When the markets are performing badly, they are said to be a "bear market."

Here are some other statistical measures of market performance:

- **Advance/Decline Line**: This is a statistical model that tracks share prices. If overall stock prices are up, then the market is advancing. If overall share prices are down, then the market is declining.
- **10-day moving Average**: This tracks the same performance as the advance/decline line, but

over a 10-day period. This provides a greater indication of short-term performance.

- **Economic indicators**: These indicators are not a specific result of stock performance but directly influence market performance. For example interest rates, consumer confidence index, consumer price index, housing prices, corporate earnings reports, and so on.

These performance indicators will enable investors to get a better idea of how the market is trending.

Impact on the average investor

When you hear that "the markets are down," there should be no cause for panic. It's quite normal for markets to fluctuate. The most important thing is to visualize market trends over weeks, months and years. If you have a short-term strategy, then looking at a six-month trend can help you gain a good perspective and where to go.

If you hear that "the markets are up," then you also need to track the moving average as getting into a market at the top may set you up for losses as the market may turn. Therefore, investors need to be keen on what market trends are and determine the best time to get in, or out, based on expectations on return.

The words thing an investor can do is ride out a market. Unless you have a long-term strategy, riding out a market will only set you up for significant losses.

Chapter 3: Investment Vehicles

In this chapter, we're going to be taking a closer look at investment vehicles. These investment vehicles are mainly issued by financial institutions in particular Banks.

In contrast to the stock market where equities, bonds and other types of securities are traded, the investment vehicles that we will discuss are issued by private banks. These banks issue certificates of deposit, mutual funds, or annuities which are backed by equities traded in the stock market.

The investment vehicles issued by private banks and other financial institutions are available to the average investor. Investing in these types of products requires a trip down to your local bank and a talk with your investment advisor. Investment advisors won't be able to provide you with insight on what the best available options would be for you.

The criteria that go into selecting an investment vehicle depends on the capital that the investor has available for investing, the expected returns on those investments, and the level of risk tolerance that the investor is willing to accept.

Based on that criteria, an average investor may negotiate one of the products that the bank has to offer them. The selection of these investment products will depend largely on the certainty of the product itself. For example, an investor might choose to invest in a shorter-term vehicle, and therefore, may choose a short-term investment such as a 30-day certificate of deposit.

On the other hand, if an investor is willing to put their money aside for a longer period of time, they may choose to take on a financial product and would go beyond the 30-day period. For instance, an investor might choose to set some money aside for a 180-day term or even for one year. A long-term investment strategy may be highlighted by the selection of long-term vehicles such as a long-term certificate of deposit.

In the previous chapter, we took a look at the stock market and focused on both the average investor and large institutional investors. In this particular discussion, we won't be looking at large institutional investors. Rather, we will be looking and the average investor and how they can set some money aside to put toward the investment products offered by a traditional Bank.

In this discussion, we're going to be considering the average retail bank that deals directly, one-on-one with customers and offers a range of products that go from savings and Loans to moderate investment products. We won't be considering large investment banks such as JPMorgan or Merrill Lynch.

It's worth noting that the money which investors will set aside toward investing in the products offered by retail banks will more than likely come from a portion of their earnings. These are surplus earning which have been saved. As such, the average investor will be more risk-averse as compared large institutional investors such as hedge funds.

As mentioned in the previous chapter, hedge funds are more willing to take on higher risk since they're seeking a higher return. Plus, the proportion of a higher risk, higher reward lead hedge funds toward seeking riskier investment vehicles. The average investor, who is more risk-averse, will be looking for safer investment instruments. Consequently, retail banks offer safer instruments for small investors to choose from. This not only enables investors to put their money to work, but it also allows a lower level of risk.

Certificates of Deposit

The first investment product that we will discuss is called a "certificate of deposit."

A certificate of deposit, as its name suggests, is a certificate issued with a specified face value. Its face value is agreed upon by both the bank and the investor. Most banks will offer a range of investments. For example, certificates of deposit will range from 1 to $1,000, $1,001 to 5000 and so on. There is no set range; this is up to each institution.

Whatever the bank chooses to offer to its customers depends on the investment strategies that both the investor and the bank are working to implement. Certificates of deposit are considered safer investments since they mature on a fixed date and at a specified rate. A certificate of deposit will have the backing of the issuing financial institution, and depending on that institution's credit rating, the certificate will be riskier or safer.

In general terms, an investor may not withdraw their investment prior to the maturity date. So, if a certificate of deposit has a 30-day term attached to it, the investor may not withdraw their money until the end of that 30-day term. If they choose to do so, the bank may stipulate that the investor must pay the penalty for early withdrawal.

Certificate of deposit offer a yield, that is an interest rate, which will be paid at the maturity of the certificate. This yield, or interest rate, is offered by the financial institution and agreed upon by the investor. It's important to note that the interest rate, or the yield, on certificates are set by prevailing market conditions. That is, whenever the interest rate that is set by the Federal Reserve and serves as a reference, will be the basis for the interest rate offered on the deposit. As a rule of thumb, shorter-term investments will have lower yield or interest rate. Longer-term investments will have a higher yield or higher interest rate.

Certificates of deposit have less inherent risk than other types of investment vehicles such as equities or stocks. Interest paid upon certificates will be lower than other riskier Investments. Much like bonds, there is an institution that is guaranteeing the payment of the certificate. For example, bonds issued by sovereign states are guaranteed to be paid by that state. So, unless a state may enter into default, the bond will be paid out.

The same goes for certificates of deposit. Unless the issuing financial institution is under risk of defaulting or going bankrupt, then it is virtually guaranteed that the certificate will be paid out what it matures.

One other important note: certificates of deposit are one of the ways in which banks finance their lending operations. The money collected from the issuance of certificates of deposit goes toward the issuance of loans and credit to other customers. One such type of certificates is called mortgage-backed certificates. Mortgage-backed certificates are specifically attached to mortgage loans. Investors who are willing to purchase these mortgage certificates can rest assured that their money is secured by the mortgages that other customers will acquire. Therefore, the interest that the bank collects, in addition to the capital lent, will be used to pay back investors who purchased the mortgage-backed certificates.

Mutual Funds

Another investment product offered by banks and financial investment institutions are mutual funds.

In short, mutual funds are a pool of money that is collected from various investors. Banks then invest this pool of funds. The funds the go toward investing in securities, for example, stocks, bonds, and other financial assets.

Since mutual funds are invested in the stock market, they are managed by professional money managers. These managers will allocate the funds into a basket of securities. For example, mutual funds may be invested in commodities such as oil and natural gas. Other types of mutual funds may go fully into stocks.

The investment strategy that money managers implement may vary according to the philosophy of each fund. If investors wish to get a higher return on a mutual fund, they may agree to have the fund invested in higher-risk securities. These higher risk securities may include corporate bonds which may be issued by companies in a riskier financial position. Nevertheless, they may offer a higher rate of return.

Other investment strategies may seek to find a more diversified approach. This diversified approach may be highlighted by investing in stocks, commodities, and bonds. Diversified mutual funds offer a better yield a reduced risk since the fund's performance does not depend on a single underlying asset. In fact, a diversified mutual fund spreads out risk and offsets potential losses of one asset with the gains from another

In general terms, mutual funds are made up by hundreds of different stocks. Therefore, mutual funds are typically diversified even if they are fully invested in stocks. Nevertheless, mutual funds will include bonds, among other securities, as a means of offsetting any potential losses from the stocks themselves.

In essence, mutual funds are like a small company. This company will take the money from investors and put it to work in the stock market. In many ways, it is similar to a hedge fund.

As noted earlier, a hedge fund is a club that takes money from investors, or members of the club, and invests that money as a pool. Mutual funds work in much the same way. Mutual funds tend to be much more conservative than hedge funds.

Thus, when the average investor buys into a mutual fund, they are actually buying a share of ownership into the mutual fund corporation. So, when the mutual fund corporation purchases shares of a company such as Facebook, the average investor is not really purchasing ownership of Facebook. Since the investor has purchased a share of ownership into the mutual fund company, that investor is actually the owner of the mutual fund company and not the stocks of the companies in which the mutual fund has invested.

There are different types of mutual funds.

The first kind is called the "fixed-income mutual fund." A fixed-income mutual fund is a type that is invested in bonds such as government or corporate bonds. Since bonds have a set yield, they offer a fixed income. Therefore, there is an expected rate of return that investors can count on when purchasing into this kind of mutual fund.

Another type of mutual fund is called an "index fund." These funds are generally attached to one of the major stock indices. For example, funds such as these may be pegged to the Dow Jones, NASDAQ or S&P 500. The return on these types of funds solely depends on market performance. So, if the market is booming, then investors can expect a higher rate of return. On the other hand, if markets are down, investors can expect a lower rate of return or even a potential loss.

Another type of mutual fund is called a "balanced fund." As I stated earlier, this is the type of fund that chooses to have a balanced approach between stocks and bonds. A balanced fund offers a diversified investment strategy which investors should consider to be safe.

One final note is that mutual funds have fees attached to them. These fees are charged for the administration of the fund. There is an annual fee which is charged for the operation of the fund. This can range from 1 to 3% of the fund's value. In addition, there may be other fees that come in the form of commissions. These commissions are paid upfront when investors purchase the fund. In short, this is the way mutual fund companies make money from running the fund itself. In addition, they will make money from the performance of the fund.

Annuities

Annuities are another type of investment offered by banks or insurance companies. They are often misunderstood since they tend to be complex in their calculation. Basically, annuities are a type of insurance which the average investor will pay a monthly or annual fee, and at the maturity of the term, the investor will receive a lump sum of money typically paid out monthly.

Just like any other insurance, the amount of money that the annuity will pay out will depend on the premium paid by the customer. Moreover, if a customer pays a larger premium, they will receive a larger payout. Depending on the annuity's term, the investor may choose to receive a lump-sum payment at the maturity of the fund or receive the fixed monthly payment.

Annuities are a typical investment made with retirement in mind. When an individual decides to purchase an annuity, they are thinking about contributing a specific amount of money, for example, every month, with the intent of guaranteeing their income in their retirement years.

One specific drawback of annuities is that the payments will last for a specific amount of time. So, depending on the terms of the annuity, payments may be made for, for say, 20 years. This means that the annuitant will be guaranteed an annual payment broken down into monthly payments for 20 years. Therefore, there is a risk that's the annuitant may outlive the number of payments agreed upon.

Another drawback of annuities is that they tend to be illiquid. The money that is deposited into an annuity may not be withdrawn until after an amount of time as specified in the terms of the annuity. This ensures that the annuity will not be insolvent, that is, will run out of money to pay all of the other investors who bought into the annuity fund.

In general terms, annuities are sold by insurance companies. This is why they function much the same way traditional insurance does. For example, life insurance is a pool of money collected by all of the customers who pay the premiums toward their life insurance policies. When a person passes, money is withdrawn from that fund, and the policy is paid out. Consequently, annuities work in the same manner.

Annuities are a great supplement to Social Security payments. In addition, it is recommended that individuals consider purchasing an annuity when they don't expect to collect social security. This is a way of putting money aside for retirement years when individuals will depend on a fixed income.

Portfolios

Investment portfolios are a collection of the different types of financial assets that an investor holds in their possession. This collection of assets can range from traditional equities such as stocks and bonds to other types of investments such as commodities, annuities or cash deposited in traditional bank accounts.

Wealthier individuals may seek professional advice from money managers who will help them allocate their assets in such a way that they generate the highest possible return. The allocation of assets largely depends on the investment strategy selected. An investor who is more inclined to a short-term, high-profit strategy will choose to allocate their assets in higher return instruments and thereby expose themselves to a higher level of risk. On the other hand, investors with a long-term strategy may seek to invest in safer investment vehicles such as bonds or annuities.

An important point to consider is the need to diversify. An investment portfolio comprised solely of one type of asset supposes a higher level of risk. For instance, a portfolio invested solely in equities such as stocks would represent 100% exposure to the stock market. Therefore, fluctuations in the market may represent considerable losses, or gains, for that particular portfolio.

A diversified, or balanced approach, will enable investors to make sure that any potential losses may be offset by the gains produced by other assets in the portfolio. This is why it is very important that the average investor become familiar with the contents of their portfolio. In addition, tracking the performance of a portfolio is vital to protecting investments against potential market shocks.

This doesn't mean that tracking portfolio should be a full-time job, but it does mean that an investor should be well aware of where their assets and how they are allocated.

Chapter 4: Day Trading

Throughout this book, we have discussed how investors may seek investment opportunities in different financial markets. We have discussed stocks, bonds, mutual funds, commodities, and even derivatives.

In order for most investors to enter financial markets, they must hire a broker to buy and sell financial assets on their behalf. In order to do this, brokers must be officially licensed to do so. Furthermore, they work for financial institutions that are duly registered and supervised by official government regulatory bodies.

However, an average individual may choose to enter financial markets on their own. This can be done through a brokerage company that offers average investors the opportunity to manage their own portfolio.

Individual investors who seek to enter financial markets may do so by using online platforms offered by traditional brokerage companies. All an individual needs to do is open, and fund, an account and learn how to use the platform. This will enable an individual to become a trader.

One such type of trader is called a day trader. Day traders are individuals who open their position at the beginning of the trading day and generally close their positions at the end of the trading day. This open and close generally corresponds to the opening and closing of a major stock exchange. For example, a trader may choose to follow the opening and closing of the New York Stock Exchange.

Some individuals have made day trading a full-time job. The reason for this is because they are able to make enough money to cover their expenses and fund their lifestyle. However, being a day trader is a highly speculative endeavor. A day trader must be keenly aware of the investment vehicles that they are purchasing when to purchase them, and most importantly, when to sell them. It's important to note that being a day trader requires knowledge, not only in the functioning of financial markets themselves but also in the investment platforms and tools available to them.

In this chapter, we will take an in-depth look at what it takes to become a day trader. But before we get into the specifics of becoming a trader, it is important to point out that this type of activity is not for everyone. Those individuals who become full-time day traders must ultimately give up their jobs in order to dedicate the time and attention needed to trade on a daily.

In addition, being a day trader is not a steady source of income. Just as it is possible to make large sums of money on great deals, it is also possible to lose a considerable sum of money. Thus, day trading is not the type of activity where you can put all your eggs in one basket. Done right, day trading can become a very lucrative activity.

So, if you've made it to this point in this book, it is because you are serious about engaging in the trade of financial assets. So, let's take a closer look at what it takes to become a day trader.

How to become an investor

The first rule to becoming an investor is having money to invest. That means individuals who seek to become investors must have some extra cash set aside for this purpose. For those individuals who live paycheck-to-paycheck, investing may not be feasible since all of their income goes toward funding their lifestyle and have very little in the way of savings.

Now, it is worth noting that it is not necessary to have millions of dollars in order to become an investor. Most financial institutions will require a minimum investment of around $500 for investing online.

The second rule to consider when becoming an investor is setting an investment strategy. The expectations of investors define investment strategies. That is, what an investor seeks to gain out of investing their money into a given financial market. If an investor is looking to get rich quick, they may choose to find high-yield investments. Of course, we have discussed how high-yield Investments also come with a high level of risk.

What the average investor seeks by putting their money to work is to generate alternative sources of income. These alternative sources of income are those that do not depend on having a job. While jobs may offer a steady paycheck every month, the potential for salary growth is rather limited. For an employee to receive an increase in their salary, certain conditions must be met. Generally, a raise is associated with a promotion or switching to another higher-paying job

Day trading may potentially lead to a situation where an investor may generate enough passive income whereby the investor will not be required to work in order to fund and maintain their lifestyle. What most investors look for in an investment strategy is being able to achieve financial security and financial freedom. This is the core tenet of becoming an investor.

Let's compare being an employee, and having a steady paycheck, to becoming an investor and having a steady stream of income as a result of investing in financial instruments.

After a certain amount of years, employees may collect a pension and/or social security. These payouts typically come after decades of work and will ensure income for an individual during their retirement years, that is, when they can no longer work. Pensions and social security are limited, and their growth potential is virtually nil. Moreover, more pensions and social security payments may not be inherited to future generations

On the other hand, savvy investing may lead to unlimited growth potential of income. Unlimited growth potential is due to the fact that wise investing is not capped off at any point. As a matter of fact, profitable Investments will not only produce income for an unlimited amount of time, but they also increase in the income generated. One such example may be a mutual fund that gains in value over time.

Other Financial assets with unlimited growth potential are stocks. For instance, if an investor owns a given amount of shares in a company whose valuation skyrockets due to their performance, this investor may choose to sell and clean up thanks to the exponential growth in that company's valuation.

The next rule to becoming an investor is related to mindset. Becoming an investor depends largely on the tolerance of risk. For those folks who are risk-averse, there are many safe investment vehicles such as certificates of deposit or government bonds. However, becoming a day trader is a riskier proposition. Therefore, a more adventurous mindset is needed in order to become successful in trading. In many ways, becoming a successful investor means that you are not afraid to take on the risks that come with making money through investing in financial markets

How to purchase funds online

The emergence of the internet has allowed the average investor to take control of their own investment strategies. In the past, an investor needed to go through a broker in order to allocate their money into financial markets. The internet, however, now offers a myriad of opportunities for the average investor the sink their teeth into.

As such, investors can use the internet, through the use of online trading platforms, to buy and sell equities. Trading platforms are offered by many of the large brokerage firms that have invested time and money into developing these systems.

Consequently, any individual with enough funds may choose to open an account in order to begin trading.

It is recommended to utilize a training platform in order to learn how to purchase financial assets. The reason for this is because an average individual may not be familiar with the mechanics of buying and selling stocks. However, the use of a training platform will familiarize new investors to the way stocks are traded. Thus, the use of a trading platform cuts out the need for a middleman.

This enables investors to take full control of the management of their fund. This is significant since stockbrokers and money managers will decide how to invest a customer's money. Needless to say, customers and brokers don't always see eye-to-eye with regard to investment strategy. Thus, being able to control investment strategies is an attractive quality of online trading platforms.

There are several trading platforms out there available for the average investor. In this book, we are not endorsing any particular trading platforms. But we are advocating the use of trading platforms in order to buy and sell financial assets. It is recommended that the average investor look into all the possible platforms out there so that they may choose the one that best suits their needs

Of course, not all platforms are created equal. Some platforms offer a lower minimum amount to fund the account but may charge higher trading fees. Other platforms may have a higher buy-in but charge lower transaction fees.

Another important aspect to consider when choosing a platform is the support that comes with that specific platform. Some financial institutions offer access to their analytics and data so that account holders may see what human stock brokers are looking at and make investment decisions accordingly.

An interesting quality of online trading is that brokerage firms offer free test accounts with their platforms. These platforms offer the real experience but do not require a monetary deposit. The investor is given virtual money to invest in the platform and make trading decisions accordingly. The results obtained from the transactions made in the free test account are indicative of the outcomes that real trades would have produced.

One very important word of caution here is to beware of transaction fees. Transaction fees are generally charged per trade. A brokerage firm may choose to charge a flat rate of $5 for trade every time an investor chooses to buy or sell. This implies that there will automatically be a $5 transaction fee attached to all trades. This is very important to take into consideration because transaction fees add up and could potentially derail the profits made on a trade.

How to purchase a tracker fund

Tracker funds are basically the same as an average ETF. Tracker funds are essentially an index fund, such as a mutual fund, and can be indexed to virtually any market in the world. In essence, the success of the fund will depend on the performance of the index that it is tracking. For example, a tracker fund that is indexed to the S&P 500 will yield a profit if the S&P 500 makes produces good results. Conversely, if the S&P 500's performance is poor, then the tracker fund may lose money.

The purpose of purchasing a tracker fund is to gain exposure to a broader base. So instead of limiting exposure to a certain group of stocks or companies, tracker funds allow investors to gain exposure to the entire Market. Therefore, the performance of the market is not solely dependent on a handful of companies. Rather, it is a measure of the entire market's performance.

Since a tracker fund is essentially an ETF, investors do not actually own any shares of any company. The actual owner of the equities is the financial institution that is selling the tracker fund. Therefore, tracker funds, or index funds, are another form of paper asset.

Tracker funds are also a form of passive investing. Since the fund is made out of a broad segment of the market, there is no individual trading of individual stocks. So, investors who purchase the fund may sit back and track the market's performance. Since the fund is dependent on market performance, there is no specific yield attached to the fund.

Index funds are also a great way of low-cost investing while gaining significant exposure to the markets. A good indicator of how well a market is performing is the market's performance over time. For instance, if a market has produced annual returns of 5% over the last 10 years, it can be expected that an index fund will produce a yield of approximately 5%. If the index fund is purchased during a bull market, that is, a market in expansion, the returns may be expected to be greater. However, if the market is down, or bearish, then returns on the fund could be expected to be lower.

One other important consideration with regard to tracker funds is that risk tends to be lower since exposure to the entire market dilutes the possibility of risk. Subsequently, index funds provide a solid investment vehicle that can produce results based on market averages while limiting risk to acceptable levels.

It is also important to consider that there are costs and fees attached to the purchase and sale of these funds. This is why it is important for investors to do their research and find out what fees are attached to these funds.

Investment platforms

As discussed earlier, not all investment platforms are created equal.

While all platforms tend to have the same characteristics, not all of them have the same transaction fees attached to them. Also, it is important to consider the availability of financial assets which can be traded on a given platform.

Thus, it is highly recommended that investors look into discount brokers who offer online investment services. These discount brokers may offer trades as low as $2 per trade. However, it is also important to find out if there are any management, or maintenance, fees attached in addition to transaction fees.

If you choose to get into FOREX trading, then it would be highly recommended to seek a platform specially dedicated to FOREX. In addition, if you are looking to invest in markets outside of the United States, then you will need to search for a platform with those capabilities.

Since I am not endorsing any specific platforms, it is vital to do research into any platform you might consider working with. Personally, I would not sign up to any trading platform that does not offer me a free practice account.

A free practice account is crucial since it will give you a sense of how the platform works before you actually risk any real money. If you can produce good results on a practice account, then you can feel confident you will actually make money on the real thing. However, practice accounts usually have limited functionality such as a short trial period. So, it is important to make the most of it while you can.

Another important aspect to consider is the type of support provided for that platform. If a given platform offers little support, then you can be sure that if you run into trouble, you will be on your own. This is one of the dangers that come with discount brokerage firms. So, if support is important to you, then you may have to dish out a few extra dollars in terms of maintenance fees in order to get support.

A good rule of thumb is to do a thorough search on the opinions of real customers on the use of a platform you are interested in. Also, you may choose to visit that firm's offices and get information from an actual human being. If you are able to connect with other investors, word of mouth reference may end up being a lifesaver.

How to determine when to buy

Determining when to buy a stock or investment vehicle is as much an art as it is science. So far, there hasn't been any single investor out there who has managed to perfect a system that can determine the right time to buy a stock or equity.

So, how can you tell when the best time to purchase the stock Equity would be?

The answer to this question depends on how closely you follow the markets. If you are willing to invest the time needed in order to follow market trends and gain a clear picture of where individual stocks are going, you can get a good idea of when to buy a based on the trend of that stock. For example, if a company is trading in a range of $100 to $110, anything in that range would be considered normal.

However, if that particular stock happened to follow below $100, and you know that this is well below its usual market price, then you can safely assume that it is time to buy. Of course, you need to understand why the stock fell below its floor, that is, the $100 price. If it's due to market forces, then you can buy on the dip. However, if the drop in the price of a stock is due to poor earnings, or problems within the firm, then it might not be the best time to purchase that stock. In fact, buying stock of a troubled company may end up costing you more money in the long run.

That is why day traders live and die by the analytics and information they have access to. You can purchase premium subscription services to financial information sources which will provide you with analytics and insights into the trends of markets, individual stocks and other investment vehicles.

Furthermore, you need to be careful not to buy when the market is at an all-time high. For example, if a market is breaking records, then you need to be very careful in which stocks you will invest. The reason for this is that when you buy at the top, there's no place to go but down. Similarly, if you buy at the bottom, there's no place to go but up. However, determining where that bottom is, is as hard to predict as the weather.

Knowing when to buy a stock, or equity also depends on your gut. You need to do research and put effort into knowing where market trends are going. But at the end of the day, there's a component of intuition that will tell you when the right time to buy is. This intuition is honed through experience and understanding of markets.

Another word of caution: be wary of those pundits on television who claim to have Insider information and are telling you when to buy and when to sell. Ultimately, these so-called experts are human and could be wrong. That is why it is important to take any financial advice you hear with a grain of salt as I've always said, trust but verify. That way, you can make an informed decision as to whether to buy and wait until the price drops further.

How to determine when to sell

Determining when to sell is just as hard as it to determine when to buy.

Knowing when to sell is an art form. Many investors make the mistake of waiting for the price to keep going up. When you understand the way investing works, you will know what a normal price for a stock or equity would be.

For instance, if a stock is trading in the range of $100 to $110, a price that is above $110 would be territory for you to consider selling. Suppose that that particular stock reaches 120. At that point, you must consider selling because if you hold, the price may come back down, and you would miss out on a good opportunity.

If you were playing a long-term strategy and you're not concerned with buying and selling every time the price goes up or down, then minor market fluctuations should not concern you. However, if you have a short-term trading strategy, then you need to sell as soon as the price goes beyond a range you have determined to be normal.

You may also hear the term "bubble." A bubble consists of investor behavior whereby they pay increasingly large amounts for a particular stock or equity. You can easily identify a bubble when prices are far higher than you have observed in the past. For example, if the stock is trading at $100, but it has progressively climbed 200, then you might consider that to be bubble territory, at which point, you must sell immediately. If you choose to hold on to the stock in hopes of making an even larger profit, you may set yourself up for greater disappointment when the price comes down, and you sell at a lower profit.

This is why knowing when to sell hinges on your mindset. Overly ambitious investors will commit the cardinal sin of holding onto stocks for too long. In a way, it's better to be a day early than a day late. I would always recommend selling at any time you are making a profit. By waiting too long, you may end up potentially taking a loss simply because you tried to time the market

Timing the market is incredibly difficult because no one knows what the top of that market might be. Financial markets are highly volatile and unpredictable. Therefore, your common sense, intuition, and experience will tell you when the right time to sell will be. If you happen to sell too soon, don't worry; there will always be more opportunities to buy solid equities at low prices.

One other important piece of advice is to avoid trying to hit a home run. Most investors dream of cleaning up in one deal. Many picture that making one deal will solve all their problems for the rest of their lives. Well those deals are out there, and they do exist, but the likelihood of making such a deal is very low. So, never regret selling as long as you make money. You can regret a sale when you lose money.

Chapter 5: The Language of Investing

In this chapter, we'll be taking a look at three important elements that make up any successful investment strategy. So far, we have discussed a great deal of information pertaining to the mechanics of investing. However, the time has come to focus more on strategy and the crucial elements that can make or break a successful investment strategy.

Often, investors lose sight of these important elements, the first of which is diversification. Diversification is a crucial factor in mitigating risk.

Also, risk management is a fundamental part of successful portfolio management. When investors don't understand risk or engage in high-risk trading, they expose themselves to potentially losing a fair bit, if not, their entire Investments.

In addition, investors' expectations play a pivotal role in the decisions they make into the investment strategy that is implemented. One measure of these expectations is the annual return on investments. As such, investors expect to earn a specific amount of money derived from their Investments.

But it is one thing to manage expectations, and it's another to deal with an actual return on. Consequently, investor expectations are contrasted by actual returns, and the difference will determine if an investment strategy has been successful or not.

This is what we call the "language of investing." And by understanding this language, you can improve your chances of becoming a successful investor. By understanding this language, you can set yourself up for success.

The importance of diversification

Diversification is an overarching theme in investing. You will hear investors talk about this term when planning their investment strategies.

But what is diversification?

Well, diversification consists in, literally, not putting all your eggs in one basket. Diversification is about spreading your investable assets across different types of Investments.

Let's consider the opposite of diversification first.

Consider an investor who has $100 earmarked for investing in the stock market. This investor chooses to put his full $100 into shares of one corporation. If that corporation is a solid company and is making money, then the chances of making money on this $100 investment will be good. However, if for some reason, the company runs into trouble and posts negative earnings reports, then the chances of losing money maybe high.

In this example, the investor is exposed to a high level of risk since investing in one financial asset means that your chances of making, or losing, money hinge on the performance of that one particular asset.

As such, diversification is about mitigating and reducing risk. When you spread your eggs out into different baskets, you're protecting yourself by determining what investments will have the best chances of making money and potentially offsetting the losses that other Investments may incur.

Let's see this diversification strategy.

The investor who has $100 earmarked for investing, chooses to break that $100 investment into four parts. That means the $25 will be allotted to each type of investment. The first $25 will go into the stock market through the purchase of equities. The next $25 will go toward the purchase of mutual funds. The next $25 will be allocated to the purchase of bonds. And the last $25 will be invested in a certificate of deposit.

As you can see, this diversification strategy looks to offset the potential losses of one asset class over the other. Let's assume that the stock market goes down. Since stocks are down, that $25 investment may now be $20. However, the performance of the mutual funds is higher since that particular fund has been indexed to a different market. The initial $25 investment is now $30. In this example, the gains of one market have offset the losses of the other. As such, this investor broke even.

Therefore, diversification is crucial to ensuring the success of any investment portfolio. One clear example of this are index funds. As discussed earlier, index funds offer investors exposure to an entire market or a considerable segment of one. Consequently, the performance of an index fund hinges on the performance of the entire market. So, if one individual stock is underperforming, the remaining stocks can pick up the slack and offset the losses of one underperforming stock.

This example of diversification offers investors a safety net. While it's true that there are always risks in any type of investment, diversification serves to reduce that level of risk down to more manageable levels.

One other key advantage of diversification is that diversification enables a portfolio to be broken up into different pieces. Our previous example highlighted how a portfolio could be broken up into four parts. So, if one part is underperforming, the investor can choose to get rid of that particular component and allocate those funds into better-performing assets. This would be virtually impossible under an investment strategy that is focused solely on one asset class, or one individual stock.

Annual return on investments

The best measure of success of an investment is what is known as "annual return on investments." Stated earlier, annual return on investment begins with investor expectations. That is, what investors expect to gain when allocating resources toward an investment. For example, an investor who sets aside $100 into a given investment will expect to gain a specific amount at the end of one year. Hence, the term annual rate of return.

However, it is important to track the real performance of an investment by determining the gain or loss of that investment.

Let's assume the following:

An investor that allocated $100 toward the purchase of an individual stock is expecting to earn a 10% return at the end of one year. This expectation is based on that stocks' previous performance and market trends. Thus, the investor expects to get $110 at the end of one year. This is known as the expected rate of return.

Throughout the year, the stock's performance has been tracked. At the end of the year, the stock produced a 10% return. This means that the investors' expectations were on par with the actual performance of the stock. Let's assume now the same stock, at the end of one year, produced a 7% return. That means investors' expectations were not met. Conversely, that same stock produced an 11% return meaning that investors' expectations were exceeded.

This example underscores the importance of managing both expectation and reality. When investors have unrealistic expectations, they may choose to engage in riskier investment practice. This is true of hedge funds playing the derivatives market.

In the derivatives market, there is ample room for making significant gains that outperform traditional market returns. For an individual investor, expected returns may be linked to the market average. For instance, if a given market has produced, on average, a return of 5% a year over the last decade, then it would be safe to assume that a 5% return would be likely.

Also, Risk plays an important factor. If an investor is looking to reduce risk, they may accept a lower rate of return on a given investment. It is important to highlight at this point that the rate of return is nothing more than the money you expect to make from the investment.

To calculate return on investment, the following formula may be utilized:

ROI = (Gain from Investment - Cost of Investment) / Cost of Investment

As you can see, this formula contemplates the gain from an investment, that is, the increase in price of an investment minus the cost of the investment itself. This result is divided by the cost of the investment. The result is expressed in percentage terms. Therefore, the higher the percentage, the higher the return on the investment.

This formula does not take into account any specific time period. And while it is a simple way of calculating return on investment, the time period which it measures depends on data that is supplied to that formula.

Let's look at a practical example:

An investor chooses to invest $100 in shares of ABC company. After one month, this investor chooses to sell his shares of ABC company. The sale price was $110. On the surface, it is easy to see that the investor has gained $10.

Now, let's apply the formula that we looked at earlier.

ROI = (110 − 100) / 100 = 0.1 or 10%

The results from the calculation of this formula show how this investor gained 10% in a one-month period. Moreover, this calculation could be done over a one-year period. So, this calculation can be done over any length of time so long as the data reflects that amount of time.

Calculation of return on investment allows investors to determine if their investment is profitable and if such investments meet their expected returns.

The results produced by the calculation of return on investment allow investors to determine if allocating their money into a given investment vehicle is worth their while or if they would be better suited investing their money elsewhere.

One other note: not all Investments have the same yield. Some Investments produce higher yields than others. Therefore, the return on investment reflects the risk aversion attitude that investors may have. Also, it is a reflection of investors' investment strategy.

Risk Management

Risk management is a crucial factor that needs to be considered as a part of any solid investment strategy.

Throughout this book, we have discussed the importance of understanding risk and taking the necessary precautions to manage it effectively. When investors are clear on the importance of risk management, they're able to take effective steps in order to make sure that their Investments are protected.

Furthermore, decisions regarding the allocation of investments are deeply rooted in the implicit risk of that investment vehicle. For investors who are more risk-averse, they will seek to invest in financial instruments that are considered safer. These in instruments include government bonds, certificates of deposit, high-quality corporate bonds or more conservative mutual funds.

Institutional investors such as hedge funds, generally seek higher returns on their Investments. As such, these institutional investors are more prone to take on higher levels of risk. Moreover, they are the first to collect when payments are due on those investments.

For the average day trader, risk as a fundamental part of understanding which equities to purchase. Day traders who have a conservative long-term investment strategy may choose to purchase equities of renowned companies which have a solid track record. These companies will not only pay a healthy dividend but will also reduce the likelihood of potential default or bankruptcy.

It is very important that day traders, or average investors, understand the importance of a more balanced approach. As noted in the section on diversification, a balanced approach enables to spread out risk over different asset classes and investment vehicles. Consequently, diversification is the antidote for investors to counteract inherent risks in any investment they choose to make.

Also, we have noted that higher risk implies a higher return. This is why institutional investors, like hedge funds or large investment banks, will choose to take on higher risk in order to maximize their potential returns. An average investor should be wary of engaging in risky trading since a bad deal could represent significant losses to their portfolio.

In addition, a portfolio that is laden with high-risk Investments may lead to a potentially catastrophic loss when a market downturn wipes out any potential gains. This may even incur in losses. In Hollywood movies, it's common to see how stock traders gamble with their investors' money on high-risk, high-reward Investments only to lose all of their money in a swift market downturn. While it is true that being successful in a venture such as this can turn ordinary citizens into millionaires overnight, the fact of the matter is that the risk far outweighs any potential gains.

Risk can be quantified through the use of statistical models. These models require large amounts of data sets in order to feed them and produce a relatively accurate prediction of where the risk lies in a particular investment. The average investor, who trades on an online platform, may have access to the statistical models which can provide information on the potential risk of an investment.

So, some general guidelines to follow about investments are as follows

- focus on historical trends of those types of Investments
- seek professional advice if you are unsure about whether an investment is potentially risky
- avoid investing in instruments, or financial assets, which you know nothing or very little about
- beware of fads. When you see that a large number of investors flocking to a particular

investment vehicle perhaps it might be time to stay away from it.

Ultimately, experience, common sense, and intuition will tell you if the risk that you are taking on in an investment will pay off in the end. It's important to note that you will never be free of risk. There is always risks in any type of investment out there. So, if an investment offers higher-than-usual returns, you must do your homework and make sure that you're not setting yourself up for significant losses down the road.

Chapter 6: Starting from Scratch: How to Grow Like the Pros

All good investors need motivation.

Often, investors are driven by the need to make a living. It is true that Hollywood tends to portray investors as greedy individuals whose sole purpose of investing is to make as much money as possible. Well, that may be true, the average investor, whether big or small, is driven by a fundamental human need to make a living for themselves.

Of course, everyone dreams of becoming rich one day particularly if this can be done without resorting to extreme efforts. Also, some individuals seek to get rich quick. History has proven that getting rich quick is as difficult as swimming across the Atlantic Ocean. That is, it is not completely out of the question, but it is extremely difficult.

In this chapter, we're going to be taking a look at some of the most famous investors in history. We'll take a look at their personal experiences and how they became rich as successful investors. From their stories, we will distill some of the most important lessons on investing.

It's worth noting that any investor who is just starting out should take a look at successful investors from the past and learn from their personal success stories. Considering that each individual is different, the point here is not to copy or mimic the actions taken by others.

The decisions made in the past were based upon the circumstances of that time. The present now has a different set of circumstances that may motivate different decisions. Nevertheless, there are general principles and lessons which are valid throughout any period in history

Through these lessons learned, new or inexperienced investors can gain a much broader understanding of what it takes to become a successful investor. The people who we will be discussing in this chapter have essentially made it rich.

Does that mean that this should be the ultimate goal of every investor?

Not necessarily. Every investor should first determine why they are even getting into investing in the first place. This will enable the development of an investment strategy. Once an investor has found their investment strategy, it becomes a lot easier to make decisions based on that investment philosophy. So, the investors featured in this chapter were folks who started off with virtually nothing and made their way up through the ranks. Their stories are meant to inspire and motivate the average investor by understanding that anything is possible.

One word of caution though: it's dangerous to compare yourself, as an investor to the big-league investors such as Warren Buffett. The danger here lies in the fact that many of these professional investors have been at this game for a very long time. They have gone through ups and downs, have had many losses, and have rebounded. Their main characteristic has been the focus and drive to stay in the market and perfect their skills.

Consequently, it is recommended that you avoid comparing yourself to other investors since each, individual investors' circumstances are different. While learning from successful investors is a significant way to develop your own investment skills, having a clear investment strategy will allow you to visualize the road map on which you have decided to travel. By keeping an eye on this road map, you will avoid the temptation of engaging in risky behaviors that may jeopardize your overall investment portfolio.

Warren Buffet

The first investor we're going to be looking at is Warren Buffett.

Warren Buffett is arguably the most famous and legendary investor in history. His holding company, Berkshire Hathaway, manages billions and billions of dollars in assets. These assets include equities bonds, private corporations, and cash Investments.

Warren Buffett wasn't born rich. In fact, he was just an average kid growing up who had a good head for business. From an early age, he was keen on building businesses and investing his money. He was known to be a very prudent teenager. The money he earned from summer jobs and after-school chores, would be put aside in a savings account. He believed that if he saved his money, he would not only have enough for a rainy day, but he would be able to invest that money into building his own business.

Buffet recalls being inspired by a book written by Benjamin Graham known as "The Intelligent Investor." This book not only inspired Buffett to become an investor but it also provided him with the general guidelines for becoming a successful investor.

Benjamin Graham, in his own right, is considered to be one of the most successful investors in history. However, his time was completely different to Warren Buffett's. Warren Buffett grew up in Omaha, Nebraska in the 1940s. Benjamin Graham had to become a successful investor in the 1920s and 30s. Nevertheless, the investment principles espoused by Graham enabled Warren Buffett to derive his own set of principles and guidelines which marked his investment strategy throughout his career.

Today, Warren Buffett is consistently in the top five of the richest people in the world. If you look closer at Warren Buffett's biography, you will notice that he is hardly a flashy and flamboyant person. In fact, he has always been a poster child for prudence and frugality. He is not the type of business person who you will see riding around in fancy cars and living in opulent mansions.

Warren Buffett's investment strategies have always focused on incremental growth. This implies that investors should not seek to find a magic bullet. Magic bullets are just that: magic. Therefore, they do not represent a true sustainable investment strategy. Quite the contrary, Buffett espouses an investment strategy that is focused on small and incremental gains. Over time, these smaller, incremental gains will compel each other to form exponential growth.

Warren Buffett is also known for his appreciation of compound interest. In short, compound interest consists in taking a specified sum of money, depositing it into an investment and allowing the gains from those investments to add up over time. Compound interest highlights how small, incremental gains can lead to larger exponential growth.

Basically, compounding works in the following manner:

Let's consider a safe investment such as a certificate of deposit. If an investor chooses to deposit $100 into that certificate, at the maturity of the certificate, the investor will receive the $100 plus the interest paid on that certificate. At this point, the investor can choose to spend the money that was produced from the investment. Or, the investor may choose to redeposit the $100 plus the interest gained from that investment into a new certificate of deposit. The new certificate of deposit will now calculate its yield based on the $100 plus the interest on that investment. Over time, the amount invested will grow and grow through smaller increments until it reaches a point where it grows exponentially. Since the sum invested has grown considerably as compared to the initial investment, we can say that the investment has compounded.

As you can see, this is hardly the most exciting investment strategy. But it is a virtually guaranteed that investors will make money. However, this is a long-term investment strategy and may not be appealing to those who are looking to get rich quick.

Considering that Warren Buffett is one of the richest people in the world, he was onto something with his investment strategy. That is why playing it safe often pays off more in the long run then rolling the dice for a short-term gain.

Chris Gardner

Chris Gardner is another of the world's most famous investors. His claim to fame came from his autobiography which was turned into a Hollywood movie starring Will Smith. The success of this film titled "In Pursuit of Happiness," catapulted Chris Gardner into investment lore.

If there was ever a rags-to-riches story, this is it. If you are interested in learning more about Chris Gardner's journey from rags to riches, you may watch the Hollywood film which chronicles his journey.

For now, we will focus on how he became a wealthy individual.

After struggling through adversity, he obtained his brokerage license. He then became a stock trader at one of New York's largest brokerage firms. Initially, he invested with his clients' money. As he earned commissions derived from his successful dealings, he took some of his earnings and invested them in his own name. His success with his clients' money, and his own led him to achieve wealth in a similar fashion as Warren Buffett.

The success of Chris Gardner's investment strategy was based upon reinvesting his gains from Investments. So, He was able to resist the temptation of having a high-flying life as a result of his new-found wealth as a stock trader. In fact, he kept a low profile for many years while he accrued a significant amount of wealth.

His track record and reputation as a successful trader enabled him to start his own capital investment firm. Gardner, along with other business partners, built one of the largest, and most successful, New York investment firms.

Gardner eventually sold his participation in this investment firm and reinvested is proceedings into assets which now fund his lifestyle. He is now a motivational speaker focusing on how to triumph over adversity and become a successful investor.

The core of his investment strategy is based on living within your means. That is, no matter how much money you make, it is important to consider that having a high-flying lifestyle is not conducive to building long-term wealth. This is a common bond between Gardner and Buffett.

Therefore, investors who seek to build considerable wealth and financial freedom must understand that maintaining a balanced lifestyle, along with prudent Investments, will enable them to become wealthy and help them to achieve financial security and freedom.

One very important common link between Chris Gardiner and Warren Buffett is risk aversion. These two investors are known for playing it safe most of the time. While there are times when you need to be aggressive, it's important to understand that playing it safe will get you to the finish line just about every time.

Another important note about Chris Gardner: his biggest motivator was to provide his family with a good life. This underscores the importance of family and providing for future generations has on the attitudes of most investors. Therefore, it is crucial that any sustainable, long-term strategy consider a balanced approach in which risk is mitigated as much as possible.

Ken Langone

Ken Langone is a traditional, old-school investor. He is an American billionaire businessman and investor whose claim to fame is financing the founders of The Home Depot.

Just like Warren Buffett and Chris Gardner, Ken Langone's beginning are humble, to say the least. He did not inherit a vast fortune from his wealthy family. In fact, he is a success story on how an individual can work their way up through the ranks of the business world and achieve ultimate success.

Langone's early career started in Wall Street as a stock trader and financial consultant. His early endeavors were focused on developing new businesses. As such, his company invested in up and coming new businesses. These investments began to grow considerably as companies became successful.

In the 1970s, Langone would go on to invent what is now known as Venture Capital. Venture capital, or VC, is a term that is used to describe individual investors and institutions who fund new start-up companies.

As described in an earlier chapter, investors who acquire stakes in private firms during their initial, start-up phase can clean up when a private firm goes public during their IPO. This is how Ken

Langone's legendary investment career took off. Among the successful businesses that his firm helped finance, The Home Depot stands out as the largest one.

In contrast to Warren Buffett and Chris Gardner, who struck it rich in the stock market, Ken Langone's career as a venture capitalist highlights the importance of having a vision when choosing the best investments out there. It is necessary that venture capitalists have the foresight, expertise, and insight to determine what startup businesses could grow and become successful companies.

Nevertheless, there is a common thread among Buffett, Gardner, and Langone. They all believe in having prudent investment behavior. This is very important for venture capitalists since investing in startup businesses poses a considerably higher risk than corporate bonds. There are no guarantees that a startup will even become profitable much less grow into a company that reaches the IPO phase.

Therefore, a great deal of restraint needs to be exercised in determining which startups to invest in. Some startups look fabulous on paper, but in reality, they lack the fundamentals that will allow them to become a successful business in practice. Other times, startups have good products or business ideas, but their founders may lack the management skills and business knowledge needed to transform a potentially successful product into a great business.

So, the moral of the story is that investors must keep a cool head whenever considering potential Investments.

Oprah Winfrey

Oprah Winfrey, who is best known as a television personality, is also a billionaire investor. She's one of the wealthiest women in the world and has proven how intelligent investment strategies can take an average individual and turn them into a billionaire.

Just like the previous investors, we have discussed in this chapter, Oprah Winfrey does not come from a wealthy family. In fact, she worked her way up through the ranks of television studios to the point where she was able to land her own daytime television show.

Most individuals would have been perfectly content by becoming a famous television personality and living off the income that comes with that status. Indeed, Oprah Winfrey made a good living for herself as a result of her talents and success on television.

Nevertheless, she highlights an important attitude that all investors must keep in mind: she was not content with the success she had achieved. In fact, she was looking to increase her investments, not out of greed, but out of a desire to achieve higher success.

Just like the previous investors discussed in this chapter, greed is not a motivating factor; rather it is success. All successful investors are driven by achieving success. Complacency is not in their vocabulary. And so, they seek to build upon past successes.

Oprah Winfrey is a good example of how Warren Buffett's prudent investment strategies prove highly successful. One such example is her investment in a company called Weight Watchers. In October of 2015, she invested $43 million into the purchase of stock valued at $7 a share. Eventually, Weight Watchers took off, and its share price went from $7 to $101. This meant that Oprah's initial investment of $43 million became $427 million.

This example underscores how understanding the value hidden away in an underperforming stock can lead to substantial gains. This is why investors must always do their homework and research new opportunities. If you look to get into a stock, or market, when everyone else is trying to get in, then you are most likely too late.

This buy-low, sell-high philosophy is one of the core tenets of all successful investors. The tricky part is being able to identify those investment opportunities. The most important factor that can help any investor achieve success in a venture such as this comes from experience and learning. This where every successful investor must take the time to put in the effort needed to master their craft. This will enable them to reach a point where they can learn to successfully identify potential investment opportunities.

Andrew Carnegie

The last investor we will be looking at in this chapter is Andrew Carnegie.

Andrew Carnegie was one of the wealthiest men in history. His claim to fame came during the Industrial Age in the United States. Just like the four previous investors we have discussed, he did not come from a wealthy family. In fact, he was the son of Scottish immigrants who came to America with nothing to their name.

He worked his way up through the business world and eventually made a name for himself in the steel industry. The steel industry was one of the industries which drove American economic expansion to a point where it became a global powerhouse. His Investments in developing the steel industry allowed him to amass a considerable fortune.

And while he is most famous for being a business tycoon, he was also famous for being a savvy investor in the early American stock market. His investment philosophy was not based on greed or ambition. As a matter of fact, he would go on to become known as one of the greatest philanthropists in American history. It is estimated that he donated about $9.5 billion of his wealth to charitable organizations.

Andrew Carnegie is a hallmark of how investing in a business can make you rich. As discussed earlier, most investors are not seeking to actively participate in the administration of a business. Most investors are looking to take a passive role by investing in businesses and thereby generate income through passive investing.

But just like Ken Langone, understanding which businesses have the potential for growth is as much an art as it is a science. Andrew Carnegie had the foresight to understand how important the steel industry would become during the Industrial Age in America. It's safe to say that if he had decided to spend his time and efforts in a different industry, he wouldn't have become the tycoon that he eventually became.

By understanding that American industrial expansion required steel, he was able to capitalize on a singular market opportunity. This exemplifies how each period in history offers opportunities for individuals to become wealthy by taking part in up-and-coming Industries and businesses.

In hindsight, those who got in early on the internet and internet-based businesses were visionaries as they were able to see how the internet would revolutionize the world as we know it. The same goes for Carnegie. He had the foresight in understanding how steel would not only enable the development of industry itself but also would become a fundamental element of the automobile industry.

The main lesson from Andrew Carnegie is that wealthy individuals are not necessarily bred in the stock market. They can also come from the business world. By understanding how businesses can potentially become successful, you can find opportunities to get in while those businesses are still in their initial phases. If you manage to get in during this phase, you can truly become rich when the business becomes successful.

Chapter 7: Governance

Financial markets, or the business world for that matter, are highly complex systems that need governance and regulation.

Now, I understand that too much regulation is not a good thing. However, ground rules are needed in order to ensure that proper functioning is ensured.

The rules governing financial markets are set by law. These laws apply to the institutions that make up each market and may vary from country to country.

In the United States, there are local and federal laws and regulations which must be observed when investing. While this book is not a guide to corporate law, we will look into some of the foundations of governance.

But first, it is important that you, as an investor, seek professional advice and legal counsel regarding your rights and obligations. It is of the utmost importance that you understand how the rules apply to you. Otherwise, you might make a mistake which may end up costing you money, or even time in prison.

That being said, governance has a dual role. This dual role applies to both investors and brokers.

As such, there are sets of rules: one set that applies to financial institutions and one set that applies to individual investors.

In general, the purpose of an individual investor is to make as much money as possible. As such, individual investors are asked to comply with the procedures outlined in applicable legislation in the same manner that financial institutions are required.

In the case of financial institutions, they have a larger number of requirements they are obligated to comply with since their activities involved larger amounts of capital and regulate potentially fraudulent activity.

If you have followed stock markets for any period of time, you can see how there have been many cases of fraud, or corrupt practices. Therefore, legislation is enacted in order to address illegal practices.

When discussing market regulation, there is a "before" and "after."

The "before" refers to the time before the enactment of the Glass-Steagall Act of 1933. The US Congress passed this act at the time in order to close the loopholes and shut down the irresponsible, illegal and even fraudulent activity that led to the market crash of 1929.

One of the core issues address by Glass-Steagall was insider trading.

Insider trading consists of executives inside a publicly traded company, who have insider knowledge of a company's financial position, exploit that privileged position for their own benefit.

One good example of the insider trading is known as "pump and dump." Pump and dump schemes are those in which company executives fudge a company's financial position by not being forthcoming with regard to the company's financial situation. In some extreme cases, executives have gone as far as forging accounting ledgers and financial statements in order to present a healthy financial position.

Consequently, stock prices for that company rise. The insiders purchase their own company's stock while it is on the rise. But since they are perfectly aware of the company's financial position, they will get rid of the stock before the company implodes.

So, the "pump" part is where insiders artificially manipulate a company's financial position, so stock prices go up. Then, the "dump" part comes when the insiders sell their stock. The unsuspecting buyers think they are getting into a great deal only to learn that they were fooled when the company goes under. When the company eventually goes under, the shareholders of that company are left with worthless stock certificates.

One great example of this is Enron. Enron was an energy company that dabbled in oil, natural gas, and electricity. The executive of that company led a pump and dump scheme that lined their pockets full of cash and left shareholders absolutely broke. The worst part of this scheme was that these executives invested their employees' pension fund in its stock. When Enron tanked, the employee pension fund evaporated.

The Enron case highlights how markets are prone to manipulation and why regulation is needed to avoid such activity.

In 1929 though, regulation was much looser. Than allowed greedy investors to manipulate prices, issuance of shares and ultimately dumping them on an unsuspecting public. The end result was the largest crash in history.

The Glass-Steagall Act also created what is now known as the Securities and Exchange Commission (SEC). The SEC is the regulatory body that oversees the regulation of financial markets in the United States. Countries all around the world have similar entities, though their size, role, and power may vary from country to country.

The SEC has played a central role since 1933 in policing financial markets.

When Enron tanked in 2001, the SEC investigated the alleged charges of fraud. The company's top executives were subsequently arrested and convicted on fraud charges.

In essence, Glass-Steagall was meant to protect all players in financial markets by outlawing one very important practice that fueled the 1929 crash: the ability of banks to become both retail and investment banks.

Let's make a quick stop here.

Under Glass-Steagall and bank could not offer savings and loans products to customers while simultaneously dabble in financial markets.

So, if a bank had retail practices, that is, offered savings and loans products to customers, they could not turn around and offer them investment vehicles that the bank itself managed. The best retail banks could do what offer mutual funds which would then be placed under the management of an investment institution.

What this separation of investment and retail banking achieved was the elimination of an inherent conflict of interest. This conflict of interest stems from a bank's ability to monopolize markets. If a bank grew too big, it could jeopardize the entire financial system if it went under.

Glass-Steagall was repealed in 1999.

This meant that banks could engage in both investment and retail activities. The end result of this was that larger banks began buying up smaller, local banks. This led to a significant concentration of banks whereby large banks scooped up more and more of the public's money.

And, this also led to the financial crisis of 2008.

In essence, the financial crisis of 2008 was nothing more than banks dipping their toes into risky investment practices. For the sake of brevity, the repeal of Glass-Steagall allowed banks to both take deposits from customers and then turn around and issue mortgages.

Given the economic conditions of the time, money was abundant in the US banking system. However, hedge funds began buying into what are called "mortgage-backed securities" (MBS). MBSs provided a solid return that was virtually guaranteed never to fail since it was backed by the mortgaged properties themselves.

Here is where the tricky part comes in.

When hedge funds realized that banks were making money hand over first in the mortgage market, they asked the banks for a piece of the score. This is where banks taped a bunch of mortgages together, got a credit-rating agency to certify them as good, and off they went to hedge funds.

The hedge funds made loads of money since the loans were high quality and the debtors paid up.

Here comes the fork in the road.

Throughout this book, we have talked about how the average investor is not driven by greed, but by the desire to make as much money as possible in order to achieve financial freedom. Well, hedge funds have no such motivation. Hedge funds are driven to make more and more money.

So, banks began loosening their screening of loan applicants and got into the now-infamous sub-prime mortgages. A sub-prime mortgage is nothing more than a mortgage given to a person with a poor credit score. Under tighter standards, they wouldn't have qualified. But under the looser conditions, they passed with flying colors. And, off went the MBSs that hedge funds fed on.

The whole house of cards came crashing down when the borrowers began defaulting on their house payments. Foreclosures piled up, and the rest is history.

In the aftermath of the 2008 financial crisis, the Dodd-Frank Financial Regulatory Reform Act was passed by Congress in the United States in 2010. Also, other countries tightened up their banking regulations in order to avoid another such crisis in other parts of the world.

Today, lending practices have gotten a lot stricter. But the underlying threat remains as banks keep getting bigger and investors keep getting thirstier for returns.

Legislation governing brokers

The previous discussion highlights the importance of having legislation that is able to regulate banking and investment practices successfully.

As a result of the examples presented, regulations for traders are rather tough. Here is a quick list of some of the current legal instruments applicable to stock traders:

- The Securities Act of 1933 (not to be confused with Glass-Steagall)
- The Securities Exchange Act of 1934.
- Trust Indenture Act of 1939.
- Investment Company Act of 1940.
- Investment Advisors Act of 1940.
- Securities Investor Protection Act of 1970 (SIPA).

- Sarbanes-Oxley Act of 2002 (as a response to the Enron scandal)
- Dodd-Frank Wall Street Reform and Consumer Protection Act of 2010.

It's worth noting that a number of provisions contained in Dodd-Frank have been repealed since its enactment. The Act still stands, but it has grown from a 2,500-page document to over 22,000 pages. Thus, the study of this Act is nothing short of a full-time job.

In addition, the agency in charge of enforcing this legislation is the SEC. The SEC has the power to shut down any financial institution suspected of illegal activities and charge individual investors of fraud. Critics of the SEC have pointed out that is has lacked the fortitude to send big-time banking executives to jail. However, the SEC has a consistent track record of bringing fraudster to justice.

I would encourage you to do your homework and read up on this legislation. It will help you get a better understanding of the waters you will be navigating in. Although, day traders are not held accountable to these laws since they are considered individual investors. Nevertheless, your trading activities will most likely go through a duly supervised financial institution. That is why it is important to have a clear understanding of where you stand.

Legislation applicable to investors

With regard to individual investors, applicable legislation is the same as that which governs brokers and financial institutions. This is why it's best to become familiar with the terms of the legislation in order to avoid making mistakes and risking severe penalties.

In short, investors need to worry about avoiding anything fraudulent or illegal. Beyond that, the best thing that investors can do is make sure that they keep good records in case anything should happen. Moreover, it's always good to check out what financial institutions you are doing business with especially if you are unfamiliar with them or never heard of them before.

I would encourage you to seek legal advice in case you are unfamiliar with anything stated in contracts or legal documentation.

One other thing: if you should ever suspect that anyone you are doing business with may be engaging in risky activities, seek legal advice. If any business associates are engaging in fraudulent or illegal activities, and it can be proven that you knew about it, you could be on the hook, too.

Tax considerations

Regarding taxes, it's best that you seek professional advice on this matter. Taxes can be complex and often require specialized knowledge. In the long run, it might be best to consult with a professional accountant or a CPA to make sure that you are complying with local and federal tax laws.

In addition, full-time traders fall under a different tax system since they are neither employees nor self-employed. It's vitally important to also plan out a solid tax strategy along with your investment strategy in order to make that you are not running the IRS afoul. Mistakes with taxes can be costly and may even result in legal trouble.

Chapter 8: How to Win the Stock Market Game

In this chapter, we're going to be looking at some additional investment strategies that can help you get ahead of the stock market game. So far, we've discussed the number of important elements associated with investment strategy. However, the four strategies that we will discuss in this chapter are often overlooked by investors.

These four strategies are designed to help you gain a clearer understanding of how you can transform the strategies which we have previously described into much more successful overall investment approaches.

As stated earlier, an investment strategy is based on investor expectations. For the purpose of this book, we're considering a much more conservative investment strategy since we do not advocate risky investment practices.

The goal of a conservative investment strategy is to enable investors to firstly make enough income to fund their lifestyle and pay for their basic needs. Once basic needs are covered, investors can move on to bigger and better things. That being said, bigger and better things can be achieving true financial freedom.

One important note is that the strategies described in this chapter are focused more on maximizing value and return with regard to the amount invested. That is, to maximize the return on investment based on the cost of each investment made.

So, let's take a closer look at each one of these investment strategies.

Value investing

The first strategy we're going to discuss in this chapter is called value investing.

Value investing consists in an investment strategy which seeks to acquire stocks that are being traded for less than their Book value. That being said, it is important to define the difference between book value and market value.

First, a stock's book value is that which is reported on a company's balance sheet. All publicly traded companies have a book value, that is, the real value of shares based on a company's balance sheet. This book value is calculated by the sum of all of the company's physical and non-physical assets. Examples of physical assets can be machinery, inventories of goods, office equipment, and so on.

Non-physical assets can include patents, intellectual property, or any other non-tangible assets included in its balance sheet.

A company's liabilities offset these assets. In other words, liabilities are nothing more than two companies' obligations or debt to be paid.

The end result of this consideration is called a company's equity. That is assets (-) liabilities = equity.

Let's consider an example:

ABC Company's total assets amount to $100. Also, ABC Company has $75 worth of liabilities. Thus, ABC's equity is $25.

Now, let's also assume that ABC Company has 10 outstanding shares. That means we must divide ABC Company's $25 Equity by its 10 outstanding shares. The result works out to a share price of $2.50. Consequently, ABC company's book value on its shares is $2.50.

Assuming that ABC Company is a successful company, it is producing healthy results and paying investors a good profit; investors will seek to purchase shares of ABC Company. This implies that ABC Company's shares are in demand and as mentioned earlier when demand exceeds supply, the price will go up.

In this regard, investors consider that ABC Company's shares are worth $5 each. This is the shares' market value. It is called "market value" since it is what investors are willing to pay to acquire these shares. In this example, ABC Company shares are worth double their book value. That is $5 market value as compared to $2.50 book value.

Now, let's assume another scenario:

We continue to assume that ABC company shares are worth $2.50. However, the shares market value stands at $2. This means that ABC company shares are traded on the market for less than their Book value.

This can be due to many reasons. For instance, ABC Company is relatively new on the market and has not caught investors' attention. Another reason might be that the company has underperformed lately and so, investors believe that it is not a worthwhile investment. This has led the shares market value to drop below its book value.

This is where value investment comes in.

A savvy investor may realize that ABC Company's subpar performance was not due to its inability to produce good results, but rather it was due to factors beyond its control, and so, investors unjustly punished ABC Company by dumping the stock.

This is a classic example of a buy low, sell high proposition.

As an investor, if you are able to spot such an opportunity, you may put yourself in the position to clean up and make a significant profit. You may have to hold on to the stock for longer than you would like to and hope that the company will rebound — however, a word of caution. If the stock falls any further, it is time for you to sell immediately and cut your losses. On the other hand, if the stock suddenly rises, it is time for you to sell immediately because you cannot be assured that the stock will continue to rise indefinitely.

Value stocks out there. Some of which were known as penny stocks. Penny stocks derive their name because share prices are worth less than a dollar each. In a broader sense, penny stocks refer to value investing. In order to find hidden gems, you will have to invest time and research into finding such hidden gems. Nevertheless, the potential gains which can be made through value investing may well offset the time and effort needed to find them.

Growth investing

Another useful strategy for investors is one known as growth investing. This type of investing consists of purchasing shares of a company and holding on to them while that company's capital, or equity, continues to grow. Growth investing requires a keen understanding of a company's internal structure and value proposition to its customers. Often, growth investing comes from companies which are underachievers or have not hit their stride yet.

Growth investing doesn't necessarily have to happen in the stock market. Growth investors may seek to invest in privately held companies much the same way that venture capitalists do with startups.

Let's consider an example:

ABC Company is in its start-up phase. The founders of this company are looking to acquire financing in order to expand their operations. And so, they have reached out to banks and venture capitalists. This first round of financing calls for an investment of $1,000. The founders of ABC Company have decided that they need that money in order to finance the purchase of equipment needed to expand their operations.

So, venture capitalists have decided to invest in ABC Company since they feel the value proposition offered by this company will ultimately pay off. In exchange for the $1,000 in financing, the founders of ABC Company are willing to surrender 25% of their company's control. In this example, 25% of the equity stake in ABC Company is worth $1,000.

Since the potential for growth of ABC Company looks pretty good, investors have decided to hold on to the stock as the company grows. Indeed, ABC Company has taken off. Sales have increased, and their name recognition has grown solid in their market.

The book value of an ABC Company stock was $4,000 when Venture capitalists bought. This can be inferred by considering that 25% equals $1,000 and that 25% is ¼ of ABC Company's total equity. So, $1000 multiplied by 4 gives us a total of $4,000.

As such, ABC Company's Book value of $4,000 at the time of the first round of investing has grown to $8,000. This growth is the result of solid business practices and organic growth as seen in the company's increased market share and profits. At this point, venture capitalists have decided that it is time to sell their stake in ABC Company and they have found another group of investors who are willing to pay for the shares according to their new book value.

Since ABC Company's capital has doubled, the venture capitalists' stake in the company is now worth $2,000. They agreed to sell and collect $2,000.

This implies that the venture capitalists have made a profit of $1,000

In this example, investors did not make a speculative investment in the stock market assuming that the price of shares would go up based on market forces. This example highlights that there is much money to be made in investing in private firms. Furthermore, publicly traded companies may offer individual investors the opportunity to buy stock directly from them. This type of transaction is a means of bypassing the need for a broker or brokerage firm.

So, it is well worth the effort to do some research and find out if publicly traded companies offer direct purchase plans, or if there are private companies out there seeking financing from investors.

Income investing

The third strategy in this chapter is called income investing or investing for income.

In this approach, investors are looking to allocate investments in such a way that Investments produce a steady income over time. Income investors are essentially looking for a source of income that will help fund their lifestyle.

As opposed to traditional stock trading which looks to flip equities for a profit and which do not represent a steady stream of income, income investors are working to make safer investments on assets which will produce income over time.

One classic example of this type of investing is real estate. Real estate investors buy properties which they can rent out and provide them with a steady stream of income at the end of every month. It goes without saying, that real estate has its own set of risks and may not prove to be as profitable as investing in equities. Furthermore, real estate requires a considerable amount of upfront investment in terms of time and money.

Investors who are looking for a steady stream of income and who are not keen on devoting a considerable amount of time and money toward researching and involving themselves in the administration of their assets can choose from a wide range of financial instrument to suit their needs. We have discussed several of these instruments. Nevertheless, we will go over them once again in order to pinpoint a solid financial strategy.

The safest income producing assets out there are bonds. The myriad type of bonds available is highlighted by the government, or sovereignty, which offers the lowest risk and also the lowest returns. Unless a country is at higher risk of default, you can be sure that a country will own up to its debt obligation and make the payment of bonds plus interest effective. In order to maintain their steady flow of income, investors may choose to roll over their bonds and collect the interest paid out by them at a given point in time.

Another type of investment that produces income on a regular basis is a certificate of deposit. Certificates of deposit produce a yield in the form of interest and may be paid out according to the terms of the investment. These terms could be monthly or annually. Furthermore, an investor may choose to allocate investable funds into a mortgage-backed certificate of deposit. Unlike mortgage-backed securities, mortgage-backed certificates of deposit are those in which banks collect funds from the public in order to finance mortgages for their customers.

Also, Investors may choose to buy stock in either public or privately held companies. The plan here is not to trade the stock when the prices go up or down. Investor logic, in this case, would be based upon the dividends produced by the company. This dividend, or yield, on each share, will provide a type of income that investors can collect annually, or at any other point in time.

Another type of income investing strategy is an annuity. As indicated earlier, annuities are a type of investment that functions much like traditional insurance. Annuities pay out a fixed monthly or annual payment at the maturity of the annuity. This is a great investment strategy for folks who are looking to finance their retirement. The only care that needs to be taken when considering an annuity is that annuities only payout for the time specified in the contract. So, if an annuity will make monthly payments for 20 years, there is a possibility that the investor outlives their annuity. Consequently, an investor may choose to delay collection on the annuity as long as possible.

Passive investing

The final type of investment strategy discussed in this chapter corresponds to passive investing.

Passive investing means that investors will allocate their investible funds into investment vehicles that will generate an income, produce dividends, pay interest, or any other type a profit in which the investor does not have any type of participation whatsoever.

The classic example of a passive investing is royalties. Royalties are fixed payments that are made during specified periods of time and are derived from the ownership of rights to intellectual property or patents. For example, book authors collect royalties on the sales of their books long after their book was originally written and published. Likewise, Musicians and artists royalties on their artistic works for many years after these works have been published.

The average investor may choose to implement a passive income strategy. Much like incoming investing, passive investing's main purpose is to provide investors with a steady stream of income. The difference between income and passive investing is the passive investing does not involve the investor in any way other than the initial investment itself.

One great example of passive investing is buying into a privately-owned company. This is commonly referred to as being a silent partner. Silent partners will provide funding for a business but will not actively participate in the management of the business in any way. Silent partners often hold seats on boards but only in a representative role. They may have voice, but no vote or they may have voice and vote but are only required to be present at specific board meetings.

Another type of passive investing through business ownership is through the purchase of franchises. Franchises are business structures that have already been set up in such a way that investors don't need to develop the business itself in any way. Franchises offer a business structure that has already been proven to be successful. Consequently, an investor will pay the corresponding fees and royalties for the use of the business model. In return, the franchise owner will collect profits derived from that business' operation.

Another great way to engage in passive investing is through the purchase of ETFs. As described earlier ETFs are funds which pool investor money and gamble in an underlying asset or security. As such, investors only need to pay into the ETF and collect their earnings at the point specified in the contract. For instance, oil ETFs have oil as their underlying asset. The ETF managers will trade in oil while the investor is not required to do anything. The ETF's earnings are dependent on the price of oil since this is the commodity which the ETF is based on.

There are myriads of ETFs available. Therefore, investors would do well to research into the different types of ETFs available and choose the one that best fits their expectations and investment approach. For the purpose of passive investment,

ETFs provide a great opportunity to buy into a fund which does not require much work beyond periodic revisions of that funds' performance.

Chapter 9: Advanced Trading Strategies

Congratulations on making it this far in the book. I must admit it's been a pretty amazing journey. I hope you have enjoyed reading this book as much as I have enjoyed writing it. A lot of time and research has gone into producing the pages that you have just read.

But hold on!

We still have one more chapter to go.

In this chapter, we will be looking at three riskiest types of investment approaches that an average investor can engage in. This is why we have left them for last.

Throughout this book, we have encouraged a conservative investment strategy. The reason for this is that risky practices require investors to have more skill and experience. Risk is an often-overlooked factor due to investors' ambition.

Nevertheless, we will be discussing riskier propositions so that you can get an idea of how you can dip your toes into a more exciting facet of stock investing.

One word of caution before proceeding: anytime you engage in a higher risk investment strategy it is important for you to do your homework and cover your back. That being said, if something should go wrong and you take a considerable hit to your investments, you may end up losing a considerable amount of money, if not everything.

With that in mind, let's move on and look into the next three strategies which can help you make considerable gains in a short period of time.

Short selling

An investment lingo, you will often hear you the terms "long" and "short."

In essence, a long position is when you own the underlying asset that is being traded.

For example, I am selling a car. I am the registered owner of the vehicle, and I hold all rights to it. Since I have chosen to sell it, interested buyers will have the assurance that I am selling something which is legally mine. Consequently, the proceeds from this sale may result in a profit or a loss to me.

On the other hand, short selling consists in selling an asset which you do not own.

You might ask yourself: how is it possible to sell an asset which you do not own?

Well, the answer is quite simple.

Consider selling a car as an example. I can sell a car which I do not own if a customer comes to me and asks me to sell their car for them. Since I own a large lot of used cars, I have the infrastructure needed to advertise the car and provide interested buyers with the advice they need in order to purchase the car.

Now, considering that I am not the legal owner of the car, the proceeds from the sale of the car do not belong to me. They belong to the rightful owner of the car. The way that I would make money in this type of deal is by charging a commission. The owner of the car and I have agreed on the sale price. From the total sale price, a certain percentage of that would go to the owner. The remaining portion belongs to me as my commission.

Just like selling a car for someone else, short selling, or short positions, are positions that investors take in selling equities that belong to another person. This proposition becomes riskier than traditional investing since it implies that the equities and securities will be sold at a given price in the market.

Short selling also implies a binding contract which holds both ends accountable for the result of the transactions made. Stockholders who wish to sell, but not sell the stock themselves, will choose to go through a broker. The broker, in this case, will go to the market and find buyers for that particular security. The binding contract between both parties holds the broker accountable to pay a certain amount of money to the shareholders. In this example, the broker makes money off the commissions derived from a profitable sale of stocks.

However, short selling gets even riskier when an investor chooses to bet that a stock will fall in price. When to stock falls in price, the investor makes money when they turn around and sell the stock for a higher price.

The issue with short selling is that investors may lose considerable amounts of money if the stock rises in value after the investor has placed a short position. At this point, an investor must immediately buy the stock and cover their position. Otherwise, if the stock continues to increase in value, the loss will become greater.

It's important to note, that investors who short stocks are essentially betting on a stock's price going down. Since these investors don't actually own the stock, they must buy it at some point in order to deliver the shares that were sold to the buyer.

This type of trading requires investors to have buyers and sellers of the shorted stock on hold so they can make an immediate transaction based on results of share prices.

Let's consider this example:

ABC Company's current market value stands at $10 a share. An investor considers that the share price will fall. This motivates the investor to put in a short position. At this point, the investor has not purchased anything yet. However, they are on the hook for fluctuations in the price of that stock.

This investor has not purchased any of ABC Company shares but sells them to another investor at $10 a share. The short selling magic occurs ABC Company's share price falls drastically. Let's assume it crashes to $5 a share. The investor has collected $10 from another buyer but is obligated to deliver those shares to the buyer. When the share price crashes, the investor will go and purchase the actual shares at $5 apiece. Subsequently, the investor must deliver them to the original buyer who paid $10 per share. In this example, the investor cleaned up because the buyer who purchased shares ended up taking the loss when the share price fell to the floor. The investor made a killing since he was able to buy the shares at a lower price before being obligated to deliver them to the buyer.

The strategy can quickly backfire when share prices go up after an investor has chosen to put in a short position. Considering the previous example, ABC Company's share price rose from $10 per share to $11. The buyer has paid $10 per share. The investor now will be forced to purchase the shares that must be delivered to the buyer at $11 apiece. That represents a $1 loss per share.

Needless to say, this strategy is very risky since markets are often unpredictable and conditions can change at any time. Furthermore, this strategy is ideal for insider trading and can lead the criminal charges.

so, if you choose to engage in short selling proceed with caution.

Buying on margin

The next strategy discussed in this chapter is called "buying on margin."

Buying on margin essentially means that an investor borrows money in order to invest in a security or an asset.

One example of this could be taking out a bank loan in order to invest in the stock market. This is typically done by people who do not have funds to invest but wish to do so in hopes that they can clean up without actually investing anything.

This is how it works:

An investor borrows a sum of money. Let's assume $1,000. The investor then proceeds to invest the $1,000 into shares of a given number of companies. The biggest constraint that an investor faces is the moment when the loan needs to be repaid. Let's assume that this $1,000 loan needs to be repaid at the end of the month. This gives the investor 30 days for the $1,000 investment to grow.

If all goes well, the investor will collect more than $1,000 at the end of the month. The investor then repays the initial $1,000 loan and pockets the rest.

An investor on margin can make a killing if their initial investment grows exponentially. For the sake of this example, let's assume that that $1,000 investment has grown to $100,000. Magically, the investor has made a profit of $99,000 in a one-month period. All the investor needs to do is return the $1,000 and keep the rest.

Now, Let's assume the worst-case scenario.

The investor borrows the same $1,000 and invests it into a series of stocks. The market has crashed, and that $1,000 investment has evaporated. Now the investor is stuck with a $1,000 debt and may not be able to repay it. In short, this is like gambling at a casino except you're gambling with someone else's money.

Investing on margin is what wiped out a great deal of investors during the market crash of 1929. Since the stock market was in a huge bubble, investors took out loans on their homes or any other assets they could use as collateral in order to invest in the stock market. Some cleaned up, and those that stayed in the market too long were wiped out by the crash. Needless to say, many investors lost everything and ended up living on the street. This led to mass suicides of investors who have lost everything.

Therefore, investing on margin is not for the faint of heart. It requires a great deal of experience and skill in financial markets. Since it is virtually impossible to time markets, it is very unlikely that investing on margin can come without risk. Considering this type of investment is essentially gambling with someone else's money, great precaution needs to be taken. In the event that an investor loses on an investment, they will still be on the hook for the repayment of the loan.

This is why the derivatives market poses such a significant risk to the overall health of the world's financial system. Many of the transactions conducted in the derivatives markets are done on margin. Often, these deals are closed with a handshake. And while there may be legal contracts that bind all parties to their obligations, they're still gambling at a stock that will rise or fall, that a company will go bankrupt, or even bet on an IPO.

As such, margin investing is not recommended for everyone, and great care must be taken in order to be as sure as possible that investments made on margin will at least yield enough to cover the margin call.

Portfolio Management

The final strategy discussed in this chapter pertains to portfolio management.

This activity is where an individual manages investments and assets on behalf of other investors. This type of activity is generally the livelihood of stockbrokers and traders.

However, individual investors, through the use of an online trading platform, may choose to pool the money of other individuals an invest it. Typically, this type of investing is done with funds from close friends and family.

It goes without saying that this is a risky activity since making wrong investments may lead to significant losses thereby leaving a portfolio manager in serious trouble. In addition, it is technically illegal to engage in this type of activity which may even lead to criminal charges.

Consequently, any time an individual engages in managing other people's money, it opens the door to a potential disaster.

Hedge funds typically invest in this manner. And as stated earlier, hedge funds tend to engage in risky investment practices. Moreover, hedge funds are clubs of wealthy people who pool their resources together in order to make money based on the expertise of a money manager. If the manager makes a mistake, it is safe to say that the investors will not be pleased.

The safest bet is to apply for a brokerage license. It requires an investment of time and effort. Nevertheless, obtaining a license can not only open employment doors, but it can give you the edge you need in order to become a successful day trader.

Conclusion

Well, we made it to the end of the line. Thank you for taking the time to go through this book.

The next step is to put everything into practice. I encourage you to look into an online investment platform which offers a free training account. With this training account, you can get your feet wet. You can feel free to cut loose. After all, you won't lose anything if you make a couple of bad deals. In fact, you will have everything to gain since the experience you will earn is priceless.

I also encourage you to dig deeper and further your learning on the topics discussed in this book. It's worth the time and effort to become a true master of the financial markets and instruments we have discussed.

One final word of caution: always seek professional advice when you are unsure about anything. Uncertainty breeds mistakes and mistakes may end up becoming costly. So, it pays to spend a couple of bucks and seek advice from qualified individuals who can point you in the right direction.

I hope that you have found this book to be useful and informative. It is the result of years of knowledge and experience which have been condensed into this single volume. I also hope that you can become a multiplier of this knowledge. Please share this information with your friends and family, or anyone you think might be interested in becoming an investor.

As always, please don't forget to leave a review. In doing so, you will be helping other folks who might be interested in purchasing this book. Your honest opinion will be greatly appreciated and useful.

Thank you once again and happy trading!

Finally, if you found this book useful in any way, a review on Amazon is always appreciated!

The Advanced Day Trading Guide

Learn Secret Step by Step Strategies on How You Can Day Trade Forex, Options, Stocks, and Futures to Become a Successful Day Trader for a Living!

By Neil Sharp

Table of Contents

Table of Contents
Introduction
Chapter 1: The Importance of Investing
Chapter 2: Stock Market Fundamentals

- Definition of financial markets
- Equities
- Bonds
- Categories of bonds
- Options Trading
- FOREX
- Performance indicators
- Impact on the average investor

Chapter 3: Investment Vehicles

- Certificates of Deposit
- Mutual Funds
- Annuities
- Portfolios

Chapter 4: Day Trading

- How to become an investor
- How to purchase funds online
- How to purchase a tracker fund
- Investment platforms
- How to determine when to buy
- How to determine when to sell

Chapter 5: The Language of Investing

- The importance of diversification
- Annual return on investments
- Risk Management

Chapter 6: Starting from Scratch: How to Grow Like the Pros

Warren Buffet
Chris Gardner
Ken Langone
Oprah Winfrey
Andrew Carnegie

Chapter 7: Governance

Legislation governing brokers
Legislation applicable to investors
Tax considerations

Chapter 8: How to Win the Stock Market Game

Value investing
Growth investing
Income investing
Passive investing

Chapter 9: Advanced Trading Strategies

Short selling
Buying on margin
Portfolio Management

Conclusion
Table of Contents
Introduction
Chapter 1: The fundamentals of day trading

Characteristics of a day trader

> **Characteristic #1: Discipline**
> **Characteristic #2: Patience**
> **Characteristic #3: Flexibility**
> **Characteristic #4: Resiliency**
> **Characteristic #5: Independence**
> **Characteristic #6: Vision**

Day trading as a full-time career

- The day trading differs from other types of trading
- Benefits of day trading
- Drawbacks of day trading
- Basics of day trading futures
- Day trading FOREX
- Day trading options
- Day trading equities

Chapter 2: Trading basics

- Bid and Ask
- Types of Orders

Chapter 3: Setting up a brokerage account

- Overview
- Fees
- Account Minimums
- Requirements
- Cash or margin
- How to open an account
- Advantages of brokerage accounts
- What to watch out for

Chapter 4: How to choose the right stocks

- Company revenue
- Earnings per share
- Return on Equity
- Assets (-) liabilities = equity
- Analyst recommendations
- Positive earnings
- Earnings forecast
- Earnings growth
- PEG Ratio
- Industry price earnings
- Days to cover

Chapter 5: The best time to trade

Overview
Market opening
Market closing
Avoiding pitfalls

Chapter 6: Reducing risk in day trading

Determining the right amount of investable capital
Setting up a stop-loss point
Working with a broker
Taking breaks when needed
Keeping emotions in check
Avoiding fads

Chapter 7: Day trading strategies

Candlestick charting
Bullish candlesticks
Bearish candlesticks
The ABCD pattern
Reverse trading
Moving average trend trading
Resistance trading
Opening range breakout
Red to green trading
Data analysis in trading
Technical analysis in day trading
The bottom line

Chapter 8: Advanced trading strategies

Gap up, inside Bar, breakout strategy
Gap up, attempt to fill, breakout
The gap up, afternoon breakout
Fibonacci retracement pattern
Gap down, fill down, inside bar, breakout

Chapter 9: Tips for completing a successful trade

Building up a watch list
Deciding on the right stocks for you
Putting an entry and exit strategy into place
Purchasing desired stocks
Paying attention to the market until the trade is completed
Selling stocks when reaching original exit points
Reflecting on trades and extracting lessons learned
Researching information for future trades
Automating trade processes

Conclusion

Introduction

Thank you for buying "*The Advanced Day Trading Guide: Learn Secret Step by Step Strategies on How You Can Day Trade Forex, Options, Stocks, and Futures to Become a Successful Day Trader for a Living!*" I greatly appreciate the interest you have taken in learning more on how you can become a successful day trader.

This book is a guide which will help you to make up your mind, once and for all, on becoming a day trader for a living.

I know that you have a lot of questions. And, I also know that you may be unsure if this is the right job for you.

The fact is that day trading has enabled many individuals to become financially independent and provide for their families while getting away from the rat race.

I know that might sound too good to be true.

But it's not.

It's a dream that many of us have had. But only a few of us have been able to make it come true. Now, it's your turn to make it real.

How can you become a successful day trader for a living?

Well, that's what this guide is about!

In this guide, you will learn about every aspect that you need to know in order to make your first trade.

Also, I have taken great care in ensuring that the information contained herein is relevant and up to date. So, you can rest assured that you will be getting solid advice on investing in financial markets.

I would also encourage you to follow up on the information in this book.

Since constant research and learning are two fundamental actions of successful traders, I would encourage you to find as many sources of information as you can in order to make informed decisions.

With that in mind, let's find out what information is available to you so that you may build a killer investment strategy.

I hope you are as eager as I am to get started.

So, here we go!

Chapter 1: The fundamentals of day trading

Day trading is just like any other career you could choose. However, not many folks understand how it works. You may have heard many people talk about how potentially lucrative it can be. In fact, you may even know someone who has made a living out of day trading.

In this chapter, we're going to be taking a closer look at how you can make day trading a full-time career which can not only pay for your basic needs and help fund your lifestyle. In addition, day trading can become lucrative enough to fund your retirement. More importantly, day trading is a means for you to achieve financial freedom and security.

So, let's take a closer look at what it takes to become a successful day trader.

Characteristics of a day trader

In order to become a successful day trader, an individual needs to have six basic traits. These traits will enable a day trader to become successful and the chief the results they are looking to produce.

Characteristic #1: Discipline

Discipline is by far the most important trait that any day trader can have. Discipline is what enables a day-trader to maintain focus during their day-to-day activities. In addition, focus is very important when market conditions are adverse.

By being disciplined, a day trader can be sure that they will be consistent in the way they carry out their investment strategy. This is very important since developing a solid investment strategy is not enough to become successful if the traitor cannot be consistent and stick to it.

Also, discipline is about establishing a routine and being able to follow through on the objectives set forth at the outset. Successful day traders are able to set up schedule and consistently carry out the activities that will lead them to identifying potential opportunities such as conducting research on a regular basis.

However, discipline isn't just about establishing a routine and following through on an investment plan. Discipline is also about having the restraint to avoid following trends and falling into psychological pitfalls. For example, a hot stock might be sought after by many investors. Therefore, discipline can be exercised in refraining from jumping in headfirst along with other investors who are driving up the price indiscriminately.

Discipline is also manifest in an investor's attitude by understanding that investment opportunities require a specific amount of research and time to develop. This approach implies resisting the temptation of hitting a home run or finding a magic bullet. Of course, there is always the temptation of trying to make one huge train that can make you rich. While that is certainly possible, it is highly unlikely.

Consequently, day traders must have the discipline to do nothing when there are no good opportunities available, and they must also have the discipline to act with prudence when allocating their resources into potential Investments.

Another important aspect of discipline is respecting the buy and sell points set forth in an investment strategy. When evaluating a potential investment, investors must be disciplined enough to purchase when the price falls to their expected level and not before. In addition, investors must exercise even more discipline in selling when an investment reaches their target sell point. As such, discipline is perhaps the most important factor when making a decision to sell.

When selling, there is always the expectation that the price of an investment may go up further. So, discipline enables an investor to sell at a point where they will feel comfortable with their returns and avoid waiting too long and possibly missing out on a great opportunity.

The same can be said about purchasing. Discipline is a great way of counteracting a phenomenon known as "the fear of missing out." The fear of missing out consists in wanting to take advantage of investment opportunities that will yield considerable results. Thus, an individual may jump into an investment simply because they must act quickly lest they miss a great investment opportunity. This rash behavior can lead to risky Investments and exposure to potential losses.

Characteristic #2: Patience

The second characteristic that we will discuss is patience.

Patience is the perfect partner to discipline. What discipline, patience is about an Investor's attitude.

Most individuals are looking to get rich quick. This is especially true when individual investors have ambitious goals and targets they wish to meet as soon as possible. And while there's nothing wrong with wanting to get ahead quickly, a lack of patience may cloud and investors judgment.

Patience is a virtue.

Patience is what distinguishes mature and savvy traders from reckless and immature ones. A lack of patience can lead investors to making poor choices regarding investment opportunities. This is true in cases where markets, or any other type of investments, are "hot." In such cases, other investors may be manipulating the price of a stock, asset, or commodity, to a point where other investors believe the time to act is now.

It is certainly possible to find yourself in a position where you must act quickly. Nevertheless, patience is a key factor in understanding that it might not be the best moment to get into that particular investment. In fact, you may have to exercise patience in order to wait for a stock to fall to the price that you have sent in your investment strategy. Likewise, you must exercise patience in waiting for a stock's value to rise to a point where you feel comfortable in selling.

A word of caution on being patient: investors often confuse being patient with holding on to an investment for too long. In this case, you might find yourself in a position where you may have to cut your losses. When you find yourself in a position where an investment does not seem likely to rebound after a string of losses, it might be best the dump that stock and cut your losses.

However, if you were considering a more long-term approach, then you may have to exercise even more patience in waiting for your investments to rebound. A good example of this is when you have invested in a mutual fund or an index fund. These funds are typically tied to a market's overall performance. Therefore, you may need to wait for the market to ride out a downturn so that you can begin to make money again.

At the end of the day, it all boils down to having a clear investment strategy which can outline the parameters by which you will hold your decisions accountable to. Patience is the trait that will enable you to keep a cool head while markets and individual assets go through the typical ups and downs that come with trading financial assets.

Characteristic #3: Flexibility

Another key characteristic that we will discuss in this chapter is flexibility.

Flexibility is one of the most important characteristics an investor can possess. Flexibility is about the attitude which, in essence, means rolling with the punches. Unlike other careers, investing in financial markets and instruments is a highly unpredictable and volatile endeavor. This is especially true when markets are under uncertain economic conditions. These uncertain conditions can become further compounded by an unclear political landscape.

This is why investors must always have an open mind. By being flexible and adaptable, investors can see the forest for the trees. They will be able to analyze and understand the data in front of them and realize where market trends are heading. In that regard, understanding data in market trends will enable investors to adjust their strategies accordingly.

Let's consider an example.

An investor has set a short-term strategy in which this investor has decided to get into an oil ETF. Current market analysis supposes that oil prices will remain stable for the foreseeable future. At the very least, fluctuations in oil prices are not expected to be significant for the remainder of the year. Suddenly, political instability has hit one of the major oil-producing countries. This implies a significant shift in the outlook for oil prices. The new outlook for oil prices contemplates a significant jump in prices.

This scenario presents potential investment decisions.

The first would be to buy further into the current oil ETF. Since the outlook is for prices to increase significantly, allocating further resources into the oil ETF would lead to further gains. This seems like a logical and reasonable investment decision.

The second investment decision would be to hold the current investment position in the oil ETF and wait for the market to skyrocket. At that point, an investor would consider selling their position in that ETF and collecting their winnings.

Both of the investment decisions presented here would pocket an investor a considerable sum of money. While the original strategy might have called for holding the opposition until the end of the year, the sudden change in oil production has caused a significant shift in oil prices. So, a savvy investor will be able to recognize the need to shift strategies and take advantage of the new developments.

Conversely, consider the decision of major oil-producing countries to increase their oil output and thereby bring oil prices down. Again, the original investment decision was to hold the position until the end of the year. Due to these new developments, an investor may choose to get rid of their position in the oil ETF at once.

The lesson in the previous example is that investors must keep their eyes and ears open at all times.

Consequently, investors must be ready to act when needed and keep an open mind with regard to adjusting their investment strategies. It's important to note that investment strategies should never be cast in stone. As a matter of fact, investment strategies should be taken for what they are: a road map which shows different ways to get to the same destination.

Characteristic #4: Resiliency

The next characteristic that we will discuss is resiliency.

Resiliency is a fundamental trait in any trader. Resiliency is key because it is part of an investor's mindset in which obstacles and setbacks will not stop them from staying on course. Resiliency is as much about being mentally tough as it is putting failures and setbacks in the past.

Trading is just like life. Life is filled with many ups and downs. The problem is not failing or losing. The problem is how you can bounce back from a negative experience. Resilient individuals will take failures and losses as learning experiences. They will derive important understanding that will enable them to be successful in the future.

In contrast, those individuals who are not resilient will allow a setback to bring them down. These individuals are the kind that starts something and leaves it as soon as it gets tough — as such, being resilient is about staying the course even when things get very tough.

However, being resilient does not imply that an investor should continue making the same trade or investing in the same vehicles when losses or adverse market conditions are clearly apparent. In fact, a losing trade may be a signal that it is time to shift focus into another stock or another type of investment. This is where a negative experience will enable them to learn an important lesson.

Furthermore, slumps and losing streaks are also common in trading. A good example are professional athletes. Even high-performance athletes will run into the occasional slump and losing streak. When this occurs, top-level athletes will go back to the drawing board and try to understand what's not working right in order to go back to their winning ways.

The same attitude holds true for investors. An investor who suddenly hits the wall and finds himself in the middle of a slump would do well to go back to the drawing board and revisit the original investment strategy. From there, important lessons learned can be derived. These lessons may include an understanding of what has changed or what's not working well. Then, an investor can choose to make the changes that they consider appropriate.

One important consideration of resiliency is that investors need not be perfect. As a matter of fact, an investor can lose half the time and still build significant wealth. The trick to ensuring that an investor will build wealth in spite of losses is to hedge risk as much as possible. That is, if a trade goes bad then the losses from that trade should not cripple an investor's financial position.

In addition, consistency is very important. A trader who consistently gets good results will most assuredly get ahead in the investment game. So, the next time you take a loss, don't get discouraged. Take it for what it is: a learning opportunity and move on.

Characteristic #5: Independence

The next characteristic we will discuss is independence.

Independence is about not depending on anything, or anyone, to make decisions. Now, this doesn't mean taking on the world alone. What it means is that an investor should be free to act on their own.

Naturally, we all need help when we first set out to do something. A good example of that is this book. You have acknowledged that you don't know everything or may need a nudge in the right direction. So, this book seeks to provide the direction you need in order to become successful at trading.

Furthermore, being successful at training is a lifelong learning process. No one will ever know everything there is to know about trading. That means there was always something new that you can learn. Based on that, you can take classes, courses, seminars, or just read as much as you can on the topic. By being independent, you will be able to process all the information around you and make a logical decision based on the information that's available to you.

When an investor is dependent on professional advice or other means and methods that will essentially make decisions for them, it would be best for this investor to surrender decisions to a money manager. In this case, the money manager will be in charge of allocating investable resources into assets and Investments they consider to be appropriate.

However, the main purpose of becoming a day trader is to gain independence and liberty of action. Unlike traditional stockbrokers, day traders do not work in an office and do not hold themselves accountable to a boss who dictates their actions. It is true that most stockbrokers have some leeway, day traders have all the leeway in the world. This is why the first characteristic in the section, discipline, is the first and foremost characteristic a day trader must possess.

Independence is also about being free to think for yourself. Many investors succumb to the opinions of so-called financial experts on television and the internet. An independent investor will be able to listen to these pundits' opinions and determine whether they are right or whether they are not.

Furthermore, independent investors will not go with the flow. They will not get into "hot" Investments just because everyone is getting into them. An independent investor will be able to determine if popular market trends are Justified or if they are just fads fueled by irrational behavior.

At the end of the day, a successful investor will maintain an independent view about their investment strategy while keeping their emotions in check. This attitude will most assuredly enable investors to keep a cool head at all times.

Characteristic #6: Vision

The final characteristic in this section is vision.

Vision is a fundamental trait that all investors must possess. This one is about forward-thinking. That is, having the foresight and recognizing where market trends are leading. Of course, no one has a crystal ball that can predict the future. Savvy investors reach a point where they can make reasonable assumptions based on available data at a given point in time.

Vision is also about seeing future investment opportunities. For example, those investors who saw the internet early on as a potentially worthwhile investment opportunity made a killing when the internet took off. Similarly, visionary investors are able to detect companies that may be underperforming or haven't hit their stride yet. When they do, they're able to get into investments at an early stage. When these investments take off, visionary investors are lauded for being forward-thinking individuals who found value where others were unable to.

This is why I always say that being an investor means keeping your head in the clouds. Now, that doesn't mean that your feet should not be planted firmly on the ground. That's hardly the case. The fact of the matter is that investors must dream. Investors must dream about what the future holds. Based on that assumption, investors can use their better judgment to identify those potential opportunities which could lead to significant gains down the road.

So, the next time you're considering making a trade, think about where that stock or asset is heading. Is this just a short-term trade that will help you pocket some cash or is this a trade that could lead to bigger and better things in the future? Whatever your answer may be, you will be able to make wise decisions based on your experience and clear judgement.

Day trading as a full-time career

Day trading is just like any other career. It requires a commitment in both time and effort en route to becoming successful at it.

What differentiates day trading from other careers is that it isn't exactly a job.

Allow me to explain.

A regular job, whatever it may be, positions an individual to trade their time and efforts in exchange for a wage. The employer purchases the talents and time of their employees so they can help achieve the ultimate goal of their enterprise.

On the other hand, day trading, while potentially lucrative, does not offer a steady paycheck. This is not the type of activity that complacent individuals may choose to engage in. If anything, day trading is filled with many ups and downs.

Despite the uncertain nature of trading in financial markets, day trading can become a full-time career. In order for this to happen, an individual investor must become successful at it to a point where they are able to generate enough income to cover basic expenses. Once basic expenses have been covered, ongoing investment activity aims to become a feedback loop in which the proceeds from successful investments feed on themselves and enable an investor's wealth to multiply.

It is very much a possibility to make day trading a full-time career. I do not advocate individual to quit their job today and dive headfirst into investment trading. This is why I recommend a more gradual approach. You can start out by trading in your free time rebuilding momentum. Once you are able to cover your basic expenses on a consistent, month-to-month basis, you might consider making this transition.

The day trading differs from other types of trading

Day trading, as its name indicates, consists an opening and closing position within one trading day. Consequently, the investor begins the trading day with a set amount of investable capital, invests the amount that the trader considers pertinent, makes trades, then closes all position prior to the end of the trading day. This means that when the trading day is over, the investor has cashed out. As such, day traders live day by day. In short, day traders carry out the ultimate short-term trading strategy.

Other types of trading include swing trading. Swing trading consists of traders who keep their positions open for longer than one day, but generally less than a few days. On average, swing trades range from 2 to 6 days. Based on that premise, short-term traders play the swings on the market. Swing traders tend to live on the edge in times of high market volatility.

Furthermore, day traders do not engage in longterm investments. This may include purchasing longterm ETFs, mutual funds, certificates of deposit, and so on. These investments would be considered longterm if they exceed one month.

In any event, day traders may purchase other longterm investment products are a means of allocating investable funds for the long run. In particular, these investment vehicles can be used toward funding retirement plans.

Benefits of day trading

Day trading offers a series of benefits when taken upon as a full-time job.

Benefits include:
- Flexibility in time and scheduling
- Freedom of action
- Option to work from home
- Option to work from anywhere in the world
- No bosses
- Ability to take time off when needed

Undoubtedly, becoming a day trader may sound too good to be true. After all, the prospect of getting out of the rat race, making a decent living, providing for the family and enjoying freedom of action are all great perks that come with an occupation such as this one.

Successful day traders are able to focus their work for certain periods of time, and then take time off as needed. Since day trading implies closing positions at the end of the day, there is no need to track investments over time. In fact, it is quite reassuring to know that you won't have any surprises when you wake up in the morning.

One other significant advantage of day trading is that you will be able to react quickly when market conditions change. Thus, if markets suddenly swing, you will be able to make adjustments accordingly. Longer-term investors made end up taking longer to react thereby exposing themselves to market volatility.

Consequently, day traders must be on top of everything when they are "on." Once they are "off," they can sit back and reap the rewards of a day's work.

Drawbacks of day trading

As with anything in life, the bad comes with the good.

Since day trading is not a job in the traditional sense, the freedom that comes with being your own boss comes without a steady paycheck. While more risk-averse folks would cringe at the thought of not having a steady paycheck every month, day traders expose themselves to risking their financial well-being during hard times.

Also, day trading may end up being a high-stress proposition during hard times. This is especially true when markets are trending downward. In addition, day trading may offer limited opportunities during a bear market or in times of recession. Nevertheless, hard times might present a good opportunity for finding hidden value.

Furthermore, day traders must exhibit the personal traits that we discussed earlier in this chapter. When traders lack discipline, patience or vision, they may find it difficult to execute an effective trading strategy. So, if an individual does not exhibit these characteristics, they will have a greater chance of failing.

One other important point to consider is your tax strategy. I would advocate consulting with a tax expert such as an accountant or CPA in order to determine what tax advantages may be utilized in order to protect your earnings. For instance, you might consider incorporation so that your trading activity is done by a legal entity and not you, personally. Incorporation offers a series of tax benefits that individuals do not usually get. This is why it's best to consult with a tax expert.

Basics of day trading futures

Futures contracts are a type of derivative in which the underlying asset of the contract is paid for in advance of its delivery. Futures deal almost exclusively in commodities though there may be futures contracts in other assets such as currency. Futures are generally traded on all major stock exchanges around the world. Therefore, futures are not just limited to one specific exchange.

Since futures deal with assets whose price fluctuates according to market conditions, keeping open positions for a longer period of time may expose investors to sudden market fluctuations. For instances, oil futures tend to be the riskiest of all.

Since day trading implies opening and closing positions in the same day, investors can avoid the ups and downs that come with leaving positions overnight. In addition, futures are often traded after the close of markets in the United States. That implies that fluctuations in Asian markets will have a direct impact of futures traded in the United States.

So, if oil futures fall during trading in Asia, an investor in North America may wake up to an unpleasant surprise. By cashing out at the end of the day, day traders can ensure that there will be no surprised at the beginning of the next trading day.

Advanced day traders may choose to keep positions open overnight. However, derivatives are the riskiest type of investment vehicles. This is why it's vital for investors to be absolutely clear on the advantages and disadvantages that come with dabbling in these markets.

Day trading FOREX

FOREX deals exclusively in trading currency. In essence, FOREX pits one currency against another. So, the rise or fall in the valuation of a currency would imply a gain or loss in another.

Trading currency is extremely volatile and can lead to considerable fluctuations in a short period of time. In particular, trading currencies of emerging countries can mean serious business. If caught unawares, an investor can be wiped out in the FOREX market.

Day trading eliminates a great deal of exposure since opening, and closing positions on a daily basis would enable investors to manage risk. For instance, if an investor invests in US Dollars and Euros, the time difference between North America and Europe can expose investors to considerable fluctuations overnight.

Trading in FOREX is a potentially lucrative activity during significant market swings. FOREX traders can make considerable profits when one currency is seriously devalued over another. Nevertheless, day traders are better positioned at reaping the benefits of FOREX trading since they are on top of market fluctuations during their trading time.

Moreover, it is highly recommended to refrain from leaving open positions overnight. This is especially true in overseas markets with a significant time difference such as European or Asian markets. When a trader clocks out for the day and goes to bed, they cannot react to any type of fluctuation. Therefore, leaving open positions unattended only exposes traders to unnecessary risk.

Day trading options

Options are another type of derivative. Options hold a stock as the underlying asset.

Options have two positions called "put" and "call." A "put" option consists in selling a stock a specified price while a "call" option consists in buying a stock at a specified price.

Options are often considered to be risky and complex procedures. Options also require traders to make solid assumptions regarding the trend of a stock's price. If properly assessed, an option can help a trader make money based on the fluctuations of a given stock. In a way, it takes the guesswork out of buying and selling as the contract only kicks in at the specified price points.

In addition, options are good for day trading since it allows traders to take on contracts during the trading day itself. This type of trade can become lucrative during periods of high volatility. During periods of relative stability, options would offer limited possibilities for day traders.

Options contracts may have longer terms, but as stated earlier, leaving open positions for longer than a trading day, even for several days, opens the door for increased risk due to volatility. Nevertheless, one huge advantage of options is that the contract only kicks in when the specified price points are hit.

If an investor purchases a stock at $10 and places a put option at $12, the options kick in when the stock hits $12. This means the investor made $2 on the trade. However, if the price of the stock falls, then the put option will not kick in, and the investor is on the hook for the falling stock. Depending on the type of contract, the investor may not be able to sell to anyone else other than the other party in the options contract. As such, options can prove to be riskier trades.

Day trading equities

Lastly, equities, or stocks, are the most commonly traded financial asset.

Equities consist of buying and selling stock of publicly-traded companies. Basically, money is made when investors buy at a certain price and then sell at a higher price. During times of market volatility, equities may represent important opportunities to make money.

Highly-coveted stocks may offer "safer" opportunities but offer day traders limited opportunities to make money since potential increases in share prices may not be as significant as expected. A day trader may choose to throw their hat in the ring in the days prior to earnings calls and forecasts. Depending on these reports, top companies may experience spikes in share prices which day traders can take advantage of.

Other types of equities which day traders can choose to seek are called Penny Stocks. Penny stocks consist in equities which have a share price less than a dollar. They may also include companies with very low share prices. These equities represent buy low, sell high potential. Since day traders open and close positions on a daily basis, day traders can "nickel and dime" their way to steady profits.

Another type of equity trade consists of purchasing value stocks. These are stocks whose market value is below its book value. With these stocks, day traders may find hidden gems that are either undervalued or poised for a rebound after a rough stretch. If done right, value stocks can provide investors with the opportunity to make serious gains. Best of all, day traders can horn in on significant gains while closing their positions once they have made money.

Since equities are the most commonly traded assets, there is a wealth of information, data, and analytics available to traders. This wealth information can be utilized in making informed decisions that would enable investors to use their judgment and intuition in making savvy investment decisions.

Chapter 2: Trading basics

In the previous chapter, we focused on the individual qualities that a trade must possess in order to become successful at day trading.

In this chapter, we're going to begin taking a deeper look at the way financial markets work. In particular, we're going, to begin with the basics of trading.

Financial markets function just like any other market. For thousands of years, markets have been places where buyers and sellers come together in order to exchange goods and services. In ancient times, markets were the scene of barter. Barter consisted of both the buyer and seller exchanging one good for another. For example, one individual would exchange corn and receive shoes in return. This was often a complicated process in which determining the proportion of corn and shoes that could be exchanged depended on a host of psychological factors.

In the modern marketplace, buyers and sellers use money as a means of exchange. This means of exchange facilitates trade whereby, both buyers and sellers, are able to use money in order to buy or sell goods and services. And so, financial markets are no different.

In essence, trading, in any way shape or form, is nothing more than trading one security in exchange for money. Money is then used to purchase another security. That security can be resold in exchange for money again. This process is the essence of trading. The outcome of all participants in financial markets is to build as much wealth as possible. This well is expressed in terms of money.

Also, there are winners and losers in all financial dealings. Nevertheless, under ideal market conditions, all investors could potentially come out ahead.

Now, Let's take a look at the basics of a trade.

Bid and Ask

When you look at stock prices, you will often see the reflection of what the market average is for that particular stock.

For instance, when you hear that a company's stock has reached $100, $200, or $300, for that individual stock. But just like any other trade, there must be a buyer and a seller. In addition, the stock market sets prices through supply and demand.

The law of supply and demand consists in both buyer and seller coming together at the market and determining the price of an individual stock based on a mutual agreement. This mutual agreement is as simple as comparing the price the buyer is willing to pay and the price the seller is willing to accept.

This is where the terms bid and ask come into play.

The buyer places the bid. The bid is the price that the buyer is willing to pay. In that regard, the bid is a reflection of the buyer's maximum price. This expected price is based on the average price of an individual stock. The buyer determines a specific price that they are willing to pay since this would enable trades to become profitable. The ask price is an expression of the seller's minimum accepted price.

I'm the other hand; the ask price is the price that the seller is willing to accept. Likewise, ask price is based on an investor's expectations and current market trends. If a stock has proven to be successful, the seller may have a higher ask price. Also, if the stock has been underperforming the seller may be willing to set a lower ask price.

The difference between the bid and ask price is known as the spread. Just like any negotiation, there will always be a difference in the buyer's expectations and the seller's expectations as well. If you have ever negotiated the price of any object, you will understand how this works.

Of course, there are times when buyers and sellers cannot agree then the deal does not go through. Most of the time, buyers and sellers are able to meet halfway and close the deal.

It's important to note that the spread is a key indicator of liquidity of the stock or security question. In other words, the smaller the Sprite, the better the liquidity. That means that a highly liquid asset will be easier to trade albeit at a lower profit.

The bid and ask price are not just limited to stocks and equities. They can be applied to Futures contracts options or even currency trades such as FOREX.

Types of Orders

In stock trading, there different types of orders that are placed when completing trades.

So, Let's take a look at the different types of orders.

The first is a market order. This type of water consists of buying or selling the stock for security. This order ensures that the action will happen but does not guarantee a specified price. When the market order is placed it will usually happen at close to the bid price for a buy order, and close to the ask price for a sell order. However, there is no guarantee that when the market order goes through it will be at a price specified by the investor.

The second type of order is a limit order. A limit order depends on a specific price to buy or sell the security. The limit orders function is to set a maximum price for a purchase or a minimum price for sale. So, A buy order would only happen if the price of the security is lower than the bid price. In addition, a sell order would happen if the price exceeds the minimum ask price.

The next type of order is known as a stop-loss order. The stop-loss order consists of an immediate sell order when a stock reaches a specified price. So, if a stock falls the stop-loss order considerably would be triggered, and the stock will immediately be sold through a regular market order.

The last type of border is noun is a buy stop order. This order is triggered when the price of a security exceeds current market price. Therefore, the purchase does not happen. A similar order can be issued to stop the sale in order to protect the profit on a stock.

Chapter 3: Setting up a brokerage account

This chapter will focus on brokerage accounts. Specifically, we will discuss the need for a brokerage account, the benefits of having one, and a way to set up one so that you can begin trading.

It's important to note that not all brokerage accounts are created equal. In fact, there is a considerable amount of research that goes into determining which account would be the best for you. That being said, doing your homework on the different types of accounts and the incentives available to you will pay off in the long run.

Traditionally, all stock trades went through a human broker. A human broker is a licensed professional who has the legal authority to conduct trades in the stock exchange on behalf of investors.

Nowadays, human stockbrokers are not exactly needed. The internet has enabled the average investor to set up an online brokerage account and begin trading on their own. Of course, the outcomes of those trades are solely the responsibility of the individual investor.

As such, a brokerage account consists of having excess to a trading platform offered by a financial institution. These financial institutions must be licensed to operate as authorized by the Securities and Exchange Commission (SEC).

Once an individual investor has set up a brokerage account, they will need to fund that account with actual money. The amount of money needed to fund an account will vary from account to account. Generally speaking, brokerage accounts can be opened with as little as $500. Furthermore, brokerage accounts enable investors to keep their proceeds deposited in that account, or they may choose to withdraw any amount of money in excess of the minimum needed to keep the account open.

The use of a brokerage account and an online trading platform are the two biggest requisites for a day trader. Without them, it would be virtually impossible for a day trader to conduct business in financial markets. They would have to become a licensed stock broker and work with a financial institution that operates in a stock exchange.

One of the biggest positives about using brokerage accounts and online trading platforms is that day traders can work from home, or virtually anywhere in the world, and conduct business in the stock market of their choice.

When shopping for a brokerage account, traders should consider all of the tools that come with that account. The brokerage account may include the use of the trading platform and access to all the analytics and data that are offered by the institution granting access to that platform.

Also, traders should look at the costs associated with the account and the use of the platform. Generally, accounts will charge a flat fee per trade. In addition, some accounts will charge a maintenance fee for the use of the trading platform and any other services that are associated with that account. In this regard, it's highly recommended that traders be aware of all the hidden costs that might come with that specific brokerage account.

If a trader is unaware of the hidden costs that come with the account they have chosen, these will add up and could potentially zap any profits that have been made through successful trades. Consequently, it pays to do your homework.

Now let's look at an overview of how a brokerage account works.

Overview

As we have mentioned earlier, a brokerage account is a way in which investors can actively trade in financial markets. License brokerage firms offer brokerage accounts. This could be through banks or other fully licensed financial institutions. Any number of securities can be traded through brokerage accounts such as stocks, mutual funds, and bonds.

Once an account has been set up by the investor, now turned trader, they are free to engage in active trading. Even though the account is operated through a licensed brokerage firm, the trades themselves are the responsibilities of the individual investor. Consequently, the investor is the owner of the assets allocated in that account

That being said, a brokerage account is nothing more than a means to invest. The account enables investors to buy and sell assets traded in financial markets. Since not all accounts are created equal, a considerable amount of effort must go into researching the best options available to you as an investor.

So, Let's take a look at some of the elements that must be considered when shopping for an investment account.

Fees

The first element that needs to be considered when shopping for an account is associated with fees. These are nothing more than the amount of money that the brokerage firm will charge for the use of your brokerage account.

In general, most firms have a similar fee structure. The actual dollar amounts that are charged for the for the account will vary from firm to firm. As such, let's take a look at the three types of fees that are usually charged by brokerage institutions.

- **Brokerage fee**. This type of fee consists of an annual or monthly fee that is charged in order to maintain the account. This fee is basically charged in order to keep the trading platform or system running. Depending on the account, this may include specialized information, research, data, and analytics which investors can use in order to conduct trades. Some brokerage institutions will choose to have a flat fee while others may choose to charge the fee based on a percentage of the account's equity or trades conducted.
- **Management fee**. The difference between a brokerage fee and a management fee is the person who is managing the account. If the individual investor is managing the account, then there will generally be no management be charged. If the investor chooses to have the assistance of a money manager, then they may be on the hook for paying a management fee. This management fee could be a flat rate charged on a monthly or annual basis, or it may consist of a percentage of the account's balance. Some firms offer a combination where the individual investor can manage most of the

account while seeking the assistance of a professional manager for other types of transactions. In that case, the investor would only pay a management fee associated with the assets the manager is responsible for.
- **Transaction fee.** Transaction fees are charged every time a trade happens. For example, when an investor buys or sells a security in a trade, it will have a transaction fee attached to it. Like in previous cases, a transaction fee may be a flat rate charged per trade, or it might be a percentage of the value of the trade. It goes without saying, that a trader who makes a lot of trades may see transaction fees pile up. That is why it is fundamentally important to keep transaction fees in mind.

Account Minimums

Another fundamental characteristic a brokerage account is known is an account minimum. Since brokerage accounts come in all shapes and sizes, account minimums will vary considerably from account to account, and from institution to institution. Some accounts may require thousands of dollars to join while other accounts may only require a few hundred dollars.

In some cases, some accounts may require a little as $500 but may have a higher maintenance fee to make up for the lower minimum. These accounts may also have a higher transaction fee. On the other hand, some accounts that have a higher buy-in may offer a lower maintenance fee and lower transaction fees.

It's worth noting that account minimums are very important to keep in mind. If your account should fall below the account minimum, an additional fee for keeping a balance lower than the stipulated amount may be charged.

A good rule of thumb is to keep your account minimum in mind in order to avoid getting hit with unneeded fees.

Requirements

Also, keep in mind that some brokerage institutions may ask investors to meet a certain set of criteria before becoming eligible to open an account with them. Basic requirements could include a social security number, being legal age, providing proof of employment, among other basic requirements.

Other institutions may require investors to meet certain criteria associated with net worth, amount of investable assets, or cash reserves needed to cover potential losses.

Cash or margin

Another key characteristic of brokerage accounts if the ability to operate on cash and/or margin. Some brokerage accounts will require investors to deposit a certain amount of funds and will limit them to trade based on the amount of funds they have available. Once funds run out, they will not be able to trade unless they add more funds to the account. When an account is set to margin, the investor will have the opportunity to trade a certain amount without having any funds in the account. The margin assigned to the account will depend on the type of account. Of course, the investor will be asked to cover that margin at a specific point. If the investor is unable to do so, then they may be hit with additional fees or even suspension of the account until they can cover the margin they have used up.

How to open an account

Once you have done your homework on the brokerage accounts out there, you can then proceed to open an account. While it is a fairly straightforward process, you do need to meet some requirements and submit some paperwork in order to get off the ground.

So, let's take a closer look at what you need to produce in order to get your account running.

- **Submit paperwork.** As with most financial matters, you will need to submit paperwork as required by the brokerage firm. Basically, you will be asked to submit paperwork in order to prove your identity, your social security number, proof of employment, a driver's

license, financial information such as net worth, or any information the brokerage institution deems necessary.
- **Complete application.** Then, you will be asked to fill out an application. This application is a written statement of all your information. This is the official document that you submit in order to request access to your brokerage account. The institution then processes the application. Processing times vary from institution to institution.
- **Add funds.** Once the application has been approved, and the account is ready to go, you will be asked to fund the account. This can be done electronically via a bank transfer, or through depositing a check.
- **Conduct research.** The next step would be to look at the investment options available to you. This may include the wide array of investment vehicles associated with the firm, or the market in general. This is where you can begin to test out the data and analytics tools that may be available to you. I recommend setting up a watch list so you can track trends before jumping into the investment.
- **Trade.** This is a big moment. This is where you complete your first trade using your new

account. Logically, your first trade will be a purchase. Depending on your investment philosophy, you may choose to close all your positions at the end of the trading day or leave your positions open and track the behavior of your investments.

The process described above seems straightforward and does not require an extensive amount of legwork. What it does require is for you to be aware of all aspects related to your new account. For example, you need to be aware of fees, account minimums and any other charges associated with that account.

Furthermore, day traders should consider a brokerage account that has a lower transaction fee since opening and closing positions in a single day may represent several trades throughout the course of the trading day. So, bear in mind that transaction fees add up and can cut into your profits.

Advantages of brokerage accounts

Perhaps the single most important advantage is that brokerage accounts offer a tremendous amount of freedom to traders. Since the trader is the only responsible for the transactions conducted in the account, the decision of where to allocate the account's funds depends on the experience and judgment of the investor.

With that in mind, it's important to consider that brokerage accounts will always have the edge over any other investment account that's managed by brokers and agents. The reason for this is that professionally managed accounts will kill you with fees. In addition, brokers will use their judgment in the allocation of investable assets. Thus, your opinion may not count for much.

Brokerage accounts also enable investors to trade when they are able to. If you, as a trader, need to take some time off, you have the freedom to do it. The account will be there when you choose to resume trading.

One other key advantage is that some brokerage accounts have a lower buy-in as compared to a traditional investment account. Often, traditional investment accounts have buy-ins in the tens of thousands of dollars.

With a brokerage account, the buy-in is a fraction of what a professionally-managed account would require. On top of that, the job that a regular stockbroker can do isn't that much better than what a day trader can do. So, brokerage accounts will allow you to reduce the management fees charged by money managers.

What to watch out for

Lastly, there are several things to keep an eye on when you are shopping for a brokerage account.

- **Full-service account or discount account**. Full-service accounts generally offer greater support and tools. You get access to all the data and analytics that the brokerage firm has to offer. This may include insider research and other specialized advice. Some accounts even offer special training sessions. Discount brokers charge less, but also offer less. In the long run, a discount broker may end up leaving the investor out in the cold.
- **Shop around for fees**. A comparison of fees charged by different firms will enable you to see the pros and cons of each account. So, it pays to take the time to do some solid research. That way, you can have a clear idea of how your finances will play out.
- **Available investments**. Not all firms trade the same investment vehicles. So, it's important for you to be sure that your chosen firm trades in the investments you are looking to deal with.
- **Resources**. Make sure that you are aware of the resources that each account offers. As stated earlier, some offer more than others. So, it pays to do research on each one.

- **Experience**. Getting reviews from other users will allow you to get a picture in your mind about what kind of experience you can expect with your chosen institution's accounts and platforms.
- **Perks**. Some brokerage institutions will offer a series of perks in order to get you to sign up. Find out what they can offer to entice you to sign up.

One final thought: you shouldn't feel married to a given account. While you may be required to stay on board for a fixed period of time, don't be afraid to switch if you need to. There are plenty of options out there to choose from.

Chapter 4: How to choose the right stocks

Choosing the right stock might seem like trying to call the weather.

Financial markets are often unpredictable, and at times, highly volatile. This is why choosing the right stocks boils down to having access to the right information and then knowing what to do with that information.

In addition, there is a myriad of indicators, variables, trends, among other dates, which you can use to make your analyses leading up to an investment decision.

The biggest piece of advice that I can give is to stick with what you know at first. For instance, if you are familiar with tech companies, then starting out with tech stocks would make the learning curve a lot more manageable for you. If you are the kind of person that is up to date on the latest gadgets and are familiar with the business implications of new technologies, then trading tech stocks exclusively at the outset may provide you with a good boost.

In addition to being familiar with the ins and outs of a specific industry, there are also a set of indicators which you must become acquainted with in order to make savvy investment decisions. By understanding this information, you will be able to get a better picture of where a specific stock may be trending.

Best of all, the indicators that we will discuss in this chapter are not dependent on specialized subscription services or any insider information. These are usually available in the mainstream business media. So, you won't have a hard time getting the information you need.

Company revenue

In order for you to make a wise investment decision, you will need to become familiar with the financials of publicly traded companies.

But, fear not. If you are not familiar with financials or aren't too financially inclined, this is a great place to start.

The first financial indicator we will discuss is company revenue.

In short, a company's revenue is all the income that a company gets. The most typical source of income for a company is sales. However, there are other sources of income such as interest paid on deposits, royalties from patents, tax refunds, among other non-sale sources of income.

The determination of revenue is the result of a company's accounting process. This process is carried out by a company's accounting staff and is reported quarterly. It is important to note that publicly traded

companies are required to present earnings reports every quarter. This is why some of the hottest tradings happen around the time of quarterly reporting. Here is a general guideline of when earnings reports are expected:
- Mid-January: Q4 (previous year)
- April: Q1 (January to March)
- July: Q2 (April to June)
- October: Q3 (July to August)

Needless to say, earnings season is always a hectic trading time since the results published a company will have a direct impact on their stock. Many investors will even purchase options in order to lock in trades based on the fluctuations of stocks during this time.

In addition, earnings reports are publicly available. Some companies choose to publish these reports on their websites. However, it is not a legal requirement for companies to do so. So, the safest bet is to check out the SEC's website. It contains links to the financial statements of all publicly traded companies.

It is highly recommended that you take the time to go over the financial statement of any company you are interested in buying. It is time-consuming, but the consolidated balance sheet, audit notes, and executive summary will enable you to get a clear picture of a company's financial position without digging too deep into their actual financials.

Earnings per share

The next financial indicator to keep in mind is known as earnings per share.

This indicator is a proportion between the earnings, or revenue, of a company divided by the number of outstanding shares.

For instance, if ABC Company has reported earnings of $10,000 and it has 1,000 outstanding shares, the then earnings per share can be calculated as 10,000 / 1,000 = 100. In this example, the earnings per share are $100 per share.

It is important to note that this indicator should not be confused with dividends. Earnings per share indicate how much of a company's revenue corresponds to each outstanding share. A dividend is the amount of money shareholders receive from the company's profits at the end of a fiscal year.

Consequently, a company may post solid earnings per share results, yet it may not pay out a dividend because it has actually taken a loss instead of making a profit. On the other hand, if a company is doing well and generating profits, investors will receive a check for the dividends they are entitled to at the end of the fiscal year.

Return on Equity

Return on equity refers to the amount of money corresponding to profits divided by the company's equity, or capital, at the end of the fiscal year.

In order to determine a company's equity, the following equation must be used:

Assets (-) liabilities = equity

In this formula, assets can be considered as anything the company owns. In addition, assets include rights a company has to collect on a debt. For example, if a company has sold "X" amount of goods on credit, the company has the right to collect on that credit. This is known as "accounts receivable," and it is an asset. Assets include vehicles, inventory of goods, office equipment, buildings, among other non-tangible assets such as patents and intellectual property.

Liabilities are essential anything a company has to pay. For example, outstanding loans and payments due to suppliers can be considered as liabilities. Liabilities are also classified as short-term and long-term. Short-term liabilities are those which mature in a year or less, while long-term liabilities mature in a period greater than a year.

The end result of this equation is equity or the company's book value.

Let's consider this example:

ABC Company has total assets of $1,000 and total liabilities of $750. So, 1,000 (-) 750 = 250.

In this example, ABC Company's equity, or book value is $250.

Now, if we assume 1,000 outstanding shares, then the stock's book value would be 250 / 1000 = 0.25. This means that each share of ABC Company has a book value of 25 cents.

Let's also assume that ABC Company posted a profit of $500 at the end of the fiscal year. So, we can proceed to calculate the return on equity in the following manner:

Profit or loss/equity

In this case we have: 500 / 250 = 2. In other words, the return on equity for this example is 200%.

This result indicates that ABC Company is in a strong financial position which ensures its sustainability in the long run.

Since you are now familiar with the calculation of this indicator, you can always run the numbers yourself to make sure that the information you are reviewing is accurate.

Analyst recommendations

I have always encouraged family, friends, and associates to take analyst recommendations with a grain of salt.

There are hundreds of analysts out there working independently or for large investment firms. These analysts will crunch the numbers based on the financials provided by companies and economic data. Based on their results, they will issue recommendations on which stocks are performing well and which ones are not.

Depending on the individual analyst of the institution they work for, they will have more or less credibility. Therefore, it is important to take analyst recommendations and check up on this information. Often, new investors will take analyst's recommendations at face value and base their investment decisions on this so-called expert advice.

If you do not follow up on expert opinions, you may find yourself exposed to risk. Now, I am not implying that analysts are wrong or manipulate information. While there have been cases of this, a wise investor, or trader, will always follow up any recommendations with their own analyses. In this way, you can determine if what you are hearing is a bunch of baloney.

Positive earnings

Positive earnings refer to the trend observed over a period of time with regard to a company's earnings.

Being able to identify this trend is crucial in making appropriate investment decisions. When you detect a positive earnings trend, it means you have found a solid company with a good track record. While it's natural for solid companies to have a down year here and there, the overall trend should be an indicator of how well that company has performed over a specific period of time.

It is highly recommended for you to go as far back as the information allows. But a good rule of thumb is to look at the last 10 years of date. This will enable you to see where the company is heading. If you detect a solid company that has had a couple of bad years, you might be looking at a company that's poised for a rebound. This may represent a good investment opportunity.

In contrast, companies with a downward earnings trend are better left alone. Unless you can get into this type of stock cheaply, buying companies like this with the hope of a turnaround may end you leaving you with a few lumps. Early on, it's best to stay away from stocks such as these. As you gain more experience, you will be able to determine if it's a worthwhile investment, or not.

Earnings forecast

This can make or break a company.

Earnings forecast are what market analysts expect a company to report. This forecast, or prediction, is based on historical data, current market conditions, and any other factors which may play in according to analysts.

These forecasts are issued by independent analysts, business intelligence companies or investment firms. The forecast issued by analysts will draw a line in the sand. Subsequently, if a company reports earnings above forecasts, then you can be sure the stock will gain momentum.

Conversely, if a company reports earnings below analysts' expectations, then the stock will most likely take a hit. The severity of the hit will depend on how bad the company missed the target.

Of course, this isn't an exact science, and there is no way to accurately predict what actual earnings will be. Nevertheless, forecasts are based on solid data and clear assumptions. So, take the time to familiarize yourself with earnings forecasts and keep an eye on your stock during earnings seasons. If analysts consider that a stock will beat expectations, then you might want to put in a position. Otherwise, steer clear of the losers.

Earnings growth

This is another indicator that tracks a trend over time. Earnings growth is a reflection of a company's management and its tendency for growth and expansion.

This trend also enables investors to see whether a company has peaked, or if it still has room to go. A flattening earning growth trend most likely means that a company has reached a peak. So, unless they are able to produce a change that will spur growth, companies may flatten and then go splat. These types of stocks will provide little to no value.

On the other hand, if you see that a company has had a decent growth trend, but has had a bad year, then you might be able to get quality stock on the cheap. You can then flip when things turn around.

This information is generally available though you could visualize trends just by looking at a company's balance sheet over the last ten years. You only have to focus on its earnings account. There is no need to focus on additional information. Of course, a more thorough analysis will lead you to look deeper into other parts of a company's financials.

One word of caution: beware of companies that haven't shown much growth and then suddenly spike. When this happens, it is usually due to singular events which have caused the company to increase its earnings. Unless the spike is part of an overall growth trend, you may have an outlier on your hands. Thus, you might want to stay away from it. Although, you could capitalize on the buzz and flip the stock while it is still up; just be careful you are ready for the next earnings season.

PEG Ratio

The PEG ratio stands for Price/earnings to growth ration.

This ratio is a measure of how well a stock has been performing as compared to its expected growth. In other words, it is a measure of how well a stock has met expectations.

This is an ideal measure for companies that have a clear growth trend. Nevertheless, it is a great way to measure any company's performance over time. It should be noted that the higher the PEG ration, the better growth potential a company exhibits.

Also, this ratio is a measure of the value of a company's stock base contrasted with its actual growth. This ratio is also considered to be more complex as compared to the traditional P/E ratio, which is, price to earnings ratio.

The traditional P/E ratio takes a company's stock price into consideration and divides it among a company's earnings. This is why the PEG ratio is more complex as it considers growth. Moreover, the PEG ratio is a much more accurate indicator of a company's growth trend as opposed to the P/E ratio.

Industry price earnings

This indicator builds on the individual P/E ratio calculated for a company and contrasts it to the industry-wide ratio. So, the P/E ratio can be calculated for an individual company and an entire industry.

The industry P/E ratio represents an aggregate measure of an industry's performance a whole. It is the sum of all of the companies in a single industry.

The industry P/E ratio can serve as a baseline for individual companies. So, if a given company has a P/E ratio above the industry average, you can be sure that this is a solid company. In contrast, if a company shows a P/E ratio below the industry average, then you may need to dig deeper to see why this company is underperforming.

It worth noting that industry averages are not entirely representative of individual companies. For example, an industry may be dominated by a single player and then made up of multiple, smaller players. This is why it's always a good idea to look at the P/E ratio of the biggest player in an industry. This will enable you to see just how wide the gap might be between the top player and other players in the same industry.

Therefore, taking a look at the biggest company will allow you to see just how representative the industry-wide P/E ratio actually is. Perhaps you might find better value within the smaller players than in the bigger ones.

Days to cover

The final indicator to consider in this chapter is called days to cover. This measure consists in determining the number of days short sellers have to cover their positions.

A short sale consists of an investor purchasing an asset and then flipping it to another buyer, hopefully, at a higher price. Nevertheless, the investor has a set amount of time when they need to pay up for the purchase of the stock.

If the short sale was successful, the investor should have enough cash to cover the position. However, if the stock should drop in value, the investor may have to sell immediately in order to cut their losses. This is why short sales are some of the riskiest investment strategies out there.

The days to cover ratio can be measured by taking the current short interest and dividing into the average daily volume. In addition, a short seller may use stop-loss orders to prevent getting hammered in case the stock they are shorting falls below their expected level.

Short sales are not recommended for longer-term investors. In fact, short sales are quite good for short-term investors particularly when a stock has seen some volatility. When shorting stocks, investors must be keen not to hold on for too long; otherwise they will be forced to cover, and they may not have the funds to do so.

Well, we have certainly covered a lot in this chapter. I know that it was full of financial discussion that you may not be familiar with. But the good news is that there are training courses that build on the concepts presented in this book.

Also, investors should become familiar with companies' financial statements. In particular, you should become familiar with balance sheets and the information they contain. Also, P/L statements, or profit and loss statements, will enable you to see where a company is heading.

Financial statements are not only readily available, but they are the best source of information on a company's financial health.

By law, publicly traded companies must present audited financial statement. That means that external auditors must independently verify the information presented by a company. Since the Enron scandal of 2001, external audit firms have been held to extremely tight standards. Thus, it is safe to assume that the information presented in a company's financial statements is as accurate as humanly possible.

So, don't fear financials. This section has provided you with the most important aspects you need to understand in order to evaluate stocks accurately. With this in mind, you can feel reassured that you have made your investment decisions based on solid financial information.

Moreover, you will be able to take analysts' forecasts and recommendations and see for yourself if what the pundits are saying in actually true. You have all the tools you need at your disposal; it's just a matter of understanding what to do with them.

To get started in learning more about companies' financials, I suggest you visit company websites. If they have no financial information available, you can peruse the SEC's website to see what information is available on any given company.

Chapter 5: The best time to trade

Day traders, by definition, open and close their positions within the same trading day. Thus, there are not open positions overnight.

We have discussed how this investment strategy can help day traders sleep better at night as they can go bed knowing that there won't be any surprised in the morning awaiting them.

Now, during the trading day itself, there are specific points in which you might see more, or less, activity. Also, there are certain points where you will notice greater gains or greater losses.

Overview

Generally speaking, markets open around 9 am. While this isn't cast in stone, it's a general rule. Understanding this is important since trades are happening all over the world while North America is getting a good night's sleep.

A good indicator of what's to come on a given trade day is the trend on the international futures market. For example, the trend seen in the futures market in Asia will help give an indicator of what to expect in North America the next day.

For those who trade in FOREX overnight currency operations in overseas markets will enable day traders to see what's up ahead for that trade day. This is why leaving positions open overnight can pose a serious risk.

Allow me to elaborate further.

Let's assume that you are trading futures. A futures contract is a type of derivative that seeks to lock in the price of a commodity in advance of its actual delivery.

The best example of a futures contract is oil. Oil is bought and sold today but delivered three months later. So technically, investors are trading something that doesn't exist yet. The oil will come into existence when it is pumped and then shipped to the refineries.

Now, if you decide to buy an oil futures contract, you may close out your day with one price point. However, oil futures took a hit in the Asian markets while you were comfortably asleep.

Bear in mind that whatever happened overnight will not affect you until the trading day starts up again. After seeing what happened in the Asian markets, investors holding oil futures and oil ETFs may choose to get out immediately. So, they are not going to wait long. These investors will dump their futures and ETFs as soon as the opening bell hits.

So, unless you are up really early, you may miss the action and see your investment plummet.

As you can see from this example, leaving positions open overnight will leave you vulnerable to the effects of overseas markets. That is why closing your positions at the end of the day will allow you to get a good night's sleep.

Market opening

In the previous example, we discussed how investors dump what they don't want right at the beginning of the trading day. Therefore, the biggest losses happen at the beginning of the day. And, the biggest bargains can be found at the beginning of the day.

Let's assume that you have been tracking a stock that's been on a downward trend. You can choose to set a price point to buy. You might even purchase an option that will trigger a buy order when the price falls to your specified point. When this happens, you could find yourself getting the deal you wanted on a stock you have been tracking.

Then, as the trading day progresses, you will find that markets tend to rebound and recover from opening losses.

The opposite is also true. When there are positive news from overseas markets, the opening of the market in North America may see a significant jump. You may choose to get in immediately and sell quickly before the momentum wears off. This might prove a bit risky since you need to time the purchase and sale quickly. This may mean that you will hold on to a position for only a couple hours, if not minutes.

So, I would encourage you to check the trends of overseas markets first thing in the morning. This will enable you to develop your strategy for that trading day.

Market closing

You might be surprised to hear that the biggest gains are made at the end of the trading day. This is true since most investors are looking to close most, if not, all of their positions by the end of the day. So, it is the last couple of hours in a trading day that tends to be the fastest and most furious.

Let's assume that you got a good deal at the beginning of the day. Since you managed to get some quality stocks at a good price, you are sitting back and tracking the momentum in that stock. Suddenly, you might see that stock beginning to climb right around 2 o'clock pm. That might be the signal that it's getting to be time to sell.

Once the stock has passed your designated sell point, it's time to pull the trigger and call it a day.

Thus, market closing generally tends to be a great time to sell especially if you are not keen on having open positions overnight.

If you are a swing trader and keep positions open overnight, then the end of the trading day may provide you with some bargains since the increased selling action may actually push the price of some assets down. This is particularly true of stocks that have been underperforming, or simply haven't bounced back. Investors who want to cut their losses or just close out for the day may choose to sell at whatever price point they can manage.

Avoiding pitfalls

The biggest pitfall to avoid has to be following the crowd. Mob mentality has led many investors to get into stocks that aren't going anywhere. Unfortunately, day traders and average investors may go ga-ga over a stock pick recommended by a television analyst. This may trigger a frenzy for that stock. Needless to say, this isn't something you want to be a part of.

In addition, having access to credible sources of information is the best way for you to make wise investment decisions based on solid data and analytics.

Day traders should also stick to their game plan. It might be tempting to hang on to stocks for a couple of days. But unless you are certain, as much as you can possibly be, that the trend observed in that stock will last as long as you anticipate, it's best to just cash out at the end of the day. It is the best thing you can do to ensure your mental health.

Chapter 6: Reducing risk in day trading

Managing risk is a key element in any successful investment strategy.

Experienced investors understand the importance of managing risk in such a way that they are able to foresee the potential drawbacks that come with engaging in any type of trading in financial markets.

So, risk is a vulnerability which leaves an investor exposed to a negative outcome. Consequently, vulnerabilities represent the potential for a negative outcome thereby creating a negative condition that will adversely affect your desired results.

Based on this logic, a risk is a potential negative outcome. That means you must do everything you can to manage that potential situation and become aware of how you can reduce the likelihood of that negative condition from taking place.

Experienced investors understand where potential pitfalls may hide and what they can do to avoid them. Often, they are aware of these pitfalls because they have fallen into them. Other times, wise investors learn from others' mistakes and are able to identify the same potential risks in their own trading activity.

In this chapter, we will take a look at some of the vulnerabilities which you need to look out for during trading. By addressing them at the outset, you can ensure that you will be one step ahead of these potentially negative outcomes.

In addition, you will begin to build your business acumen to a point where you can automatically detect when you are exposing yourself to risk.

Now, we have address risk throughout this book so far. This is why I have advocated the validity of becoming a day trader.

Why?

Well, I have underscored numerous times how vulnerable you become when you leave positions open overnight. By closing your positions before the end of the trading day, you have managed risk in such a way that you take the uncertainty away from your investment.

By opening and closing your positions every day, you are certain of what your current situation is at all times. In a way, it's providing peace of mind for yourself. So, if you had a bad day, you can put it behind you and move on. If you had a good idea, you can build on that success and keep rolling the next day.

Whatever your circumstance, leaving open positions unattended is opening the door for trouble. This highlights the biggest risk that could ever affect you: not being able to react in time to changing market conditions.

If you are not physically able to deal with situations as they happen, then you are setting yourself up for potential losses.

Let's consider an example:

You are trading FOREX.

FOREX is highly volatile, meaning that fluctuations can happen unexpectedly and can hammer you without prejudice.

So, let's say that you are trading US dollars and Euros. This currency pair seems harmless enough as neither currency has been experiencing significant fluctuations. As such, the spread margins are rather narrow. That means that your gains, or losses, won't be significant, but given the right timing, you can make a few bucks on each trade.

Now, let's assume that you open and close your position every day. Whatever your outcome, win or lose, you are clear on what your position is.

However, you decide that these two currencies are stable enough for you to leave your position open and allow market fluctuations to play overnight. You can always resume trading when you wake up in the morning. Unless you are planning on sleeping for four hours, this leaves you vulnerable to the fluctuations of European markets which trade overnight.

Let's assume further that the European Central Bank has announced an interest rate and investors begin dumping the Euro in favor of other currencies such as the Swiss Franc, US dollar, or even gold. If you are holding Euros, the value of your investment can fall rapidly zapping any potential gains. If you were at your trading station when the news broke, you could react quickly and make the trade accordingly. But since you are getting a good night's sleep, your reactions may come too late.

This example shows how things can quickly change and leave little time to react.

As a result, taking a proactive approach in dealing with risk will enable you to better protect yourself against potential risk while cutting your losses should things get that far.

Determining the right amount of investable capital

Determining the amount of money you should put toward trading is about as tricky as trying to decide how much money you should gamble away in Las Vegas.

The easiest part is understanding that you shouldn't bet the farm. Often, investors seek not to just hit a home run, but a grand slam.

As I've mentioned earlier, it is possible to hit a grand slam and clean up. It is possible though it rarely happens. The reason for this is that you would need to invest a considerable amount of capital and have the profit on a trade be such that it multiplies your original investment.

That being said, putting the entirety of your investable assets into trading all at once exposes you to unnecessary risk. Now, I am not saying that you will lose all your money and end up broke. But it should be noted that such things do happen when investors get reckless.

I have always advocated a gradual approach in which you can build up your equity at a moderate pace. In doing this, you will ensure that whatever market conditions prevail, you will not lose the farm should the worst happen.

So, I would encourage you to look at the account minimums that brokerage accounts require you to put down. Based on that, you can decide which amount you are willing to gamble away. The way I see it, think of the money you are going to invest as the amount of money you would be willing to blow in Las Vegas. That is, assume that you are going to spend a weekend at a casino, and you are perfectly fine in blowing that money on the experience of playing at a casino.

When you keep that attitude, you are not emotionally invested in the outcome of your trades. You will not feel pressure to succeed since you are comfortable with the idea of losing the money.

Does that mean that you should play to lose?

Of course not!

It just means that if you invest a considerable sum of money, you will feel the pressure to win every trade. Consequently, being under that kind of pressure may cloud your judgment and lead you to make trades that you might not be entirely comfortable simply because there is a lot at stake.

That is why I always encourage folks to avoid betting too much, too soon. If you are completely new to this game, small, incremental steps will ensure that you will have a solid strategy. Eventually, you will be able to build up enough equity so that you can engage in larger trades. As you gain experience and recognize the opportunities available to you, you will be able to hit home runs consistently. After all, the best home run hitters don't start out hitting the ball out of the ballpark. They have to strike out a few times before getting the big hits.

Setting up a stop-loss point

We discussed stop-loss points earlier when referring to the types of orders available in investing.

A stop-loss point basically consists in drawing a line in the sand in which you decided that when the stock hits that point, you will automatically sell.

A conservative approach might be to set up your stop-loss point slightly above your purchase price. Therefore, you will ensure that you won't lose money on the deal even if it means making a slight profit. Also, you could go even lower and set your stop-loss point at your purchase price so that you break even.

This approach is set to ensure that you don't lose money on deals. However, you could be a bit more aggressive and set your stop-loss point below your purchase price. The reason for this is that it will give you a bit more time for the stock to rebound even if it's trending downward. The logic behind this approach is that if a stock falls low enough it will trigger multiple sell points and the stock will rebound.

This is a risky approach since there is no sure-fire way of knowing how far a stock would fall. In fact, if you set your stop-loss point too low, it could fall below the stop-loss points of other investors. This means that you will never recoup since a large amount of sell orders will drive the price of the stock further down. By the time your sell order kicks in, you'll have a 50/50 chance, at best, to catch the rebound.

So, when deciding to set your stop-loss point always ask yourself how low you are willing to go? The answer to that question will determine your stop-loss point.

Working with a broker

Financial firms employ brokers to be full-time managers for their client's assets. As such, brokers are experienced individuals who have a clear understanding of how trading works, the risks and the opportunities that may become available to investors.

Passive investors are always willing to pay a bit extra for qualified brokers who have a solid track record in asset management. This is something important to consider especially if you are new to the investing game.

By working with a broker, you are not admitting that you can't do it yourself. What you are recognizing is that the broker's experience will help you reduce the risk of losing money while you learn the ropes of the markets. Consequently, seeking their advice can as much a learning experience as a way of protecting yourself.

Naturally, this advice doesn't come for free. However, you may want to look at what your brokerage account includes. Full-service accounts may include advisory sessions with a licensed broker who can assist you in making the right deals. This is usually part of the maintenance fee you pay for your account.

Other full-service brokerage accounts offer training seminars, webinars, or even one on one coaching calls. So, it pays to look into a full-service brokerage account.

On the flip side, discount accounts will most assuredly not offer any type of support. In that case, you may want to seek out professional advice on an hourly rate. This will ensure you the coaching you need and provide you with direct access to an experienced, licensed professional.

One word of advice regarding online training courses: online courses by so-called experts are not always 100% accurate. While they may not be intentionally misleading, they may be off in their assessment of financial dealings. Therefore, it is always a good idea to consult with different sources before heeding any financial advice. One good rule of thumb to follow is to make sure that anyone who is giving you financial advice is a licensed broker. If they give you the wrong advice intentionally, the will lose their license. So, beware of anyone who is not duly licensed.

Taking breaks when needed

Taking a break is not a risk in itself. The risk is pushing yourself too hard.

When investors take day trading on as a full-time occupation, discipline is needed in order to keep a balanced schedule. Some traders may choose to log on right at the start of the trading day, take a break for lunch and then jump into the afternoon session.

However, being a day trader doesn't stop there. There is a considerable amount of time and effort that needs to be put into research and study. This is where becoming a trader can get overwhelming. That is why keeping a healthy schedule can ensure that you will always have a fresh mind.

Nevertheless, there is a point where you need to take a break from it all. Finding the right time to do so can become challenging. Since your livelihood will depend on the results you are able to produce from trading, you will need to make sure that you have enough money set aside to cover your expenses while you are not trading.

When you become truly successful, you will be able to save up some money for such occasions. Some traders choose to take a couple of days off here and there just to unwind and clear their minds. Since markets are open from Monday to Friday, you can close your positions on Friday evening and close the shop for the weekend.

There is something to be said about taking long vacations as a day trader. sBeside the fact that you may not be producing any income when you are on vacation, being away for too long may disrupt your mojo. Now, this doesn't mean that you shouldn't take a vacation at all, it just means that even if you take a break, you would do well not to take your eye off the ball.

The good thing about day trading is that you can essentially do it from anywhere in the world so long as you have an internet connection. Thus, you could potentially go on an extended holiday and plan your trading day around other activities you wish to do or places you are planning to see.

Remember that one of the main reasons why investors become day traders is so that they can have the freedom and the flexibility to work anywhere at any time.

Keeping emotions in check

Hollywood films often portray stock traders as flashy and flamboyant individuals who wear their hearts on their sleeves.

The truth is that being a stock trader requires individuals to have nerves of steel. Often, there are situations in which traders need to keep a cool head while exercising sound judgment. Those individuals who let their emotions get the better of them may end up making ill-advised decisions regarding their investments.

Keeping emotions in check is part of the self-discipline that traders must exercise. Self-restraint is important particularly when emotions run high during bull runs or crashes. Many investors get caught up in the frenzy when other investors are clamoring to buy or sell.

In particular, market crashes tend to bring out the worst in people.

Take the market crash of 1929. Many investors lost everything but the shirt on their backs. This devastating situation motivated the suicide of ruined individuals. Fast forward to 2008, and the great financial crisis was an exercise in greed by bankers and investors while ordinary citizens got caught up in the cheap money available to them.

These are examples of how emotions can cloud an individual's better judgment. Consequently, one of the most fundamental traits of any investor is to keep their head during times of euphoria and hardship. By setting stop-loss point, or placing options are automatic devices which investors can use to protect their positions from unexpected swings.

One other important aspect, investors who are able to keep their cool will learn to see value and opportunity under circumstances when others are panicking. Furthermore, panicked investors make rash decisions. These are the conditions which savvy investors can exploit to their advantage.

Avoiding fads

Fads and trends are dangerous. Investors who follow the crowd often expose themselves to unnecessary risk. When investors choose to get into an investment vehicle when it's "hot," it means that the opportunity to make money on that investment in long gone.

Since the price of investments is driven by supply and demand, inflated asset prices occur when a large number of buyers decide to get in. At this point, the original investors have already cleaned up. What's left is a string of investors chasing the same nickel.

The best time to get into investments is in the early stages. For instance, when companies are in their startup phase provides the best opportunity for investors and venture capitalists to get the most value for their buck. When companies eventually make it to their initial public offering (IPO), these initial investors can clean up when the next round of investors gobble up the stock. Even those investors who pounce on the IPO can clean up when the stock's price gains momentum. By this point, the more recent investors will make a pittance on it.

The moral of this story is that great value can be found when investors go against the tide. When an investor decides to follow the crowd, they are only feeding the frenzy. When an investor chooses an alternative path, the opportunities for finding hidden gems increase significantly. Of course, this requires greater research, but the potential upside is definitely worth it.

In addition, investors who keep their emotions in check will be able to extricate themselves from market fads and make wise investment decisions based on their personal investment strategy while focusing on achieving their individual goals.

The points described above allow investors to manage risk. It is clear that risk is an inherent part of investing. So, there is no way to avoid it completely. The best investors can do is manage risk in such a way that there is a clear strategy defined in case the worst should ever happen.

At the end of the day, experience is the best teacher. Those investors who learn from their mistakes, and those of others, can gain valuable skills in managing risk and protecting their assets. Moreover, keeping a cool head is the best way that investors can reduce their exposure to risk. When investors do not exercise restraint in their actions, their better judgment becomes clouded. This impaired judgement can lead to making a riskier investment. As we have discussed earlier, riskier investments expose investors to even more risk. Unless an investor is experienced and fully comprehends the mechanics of the investment vehicle, it's best to play it safe. Inexperienced investors may be able to dive into the deep end as they gain experience and build momentum.

Chapter 7: Day trading strategies

Becoming a successful trader is part art and part science.

The artistic side trading consists in developing and intuition for potential opportunities and being able to sniff out hidden gems where others may not be able to find them. This artistic ability is developed through years of experience and lessons learned. Often, investors rely on their instincts in order to figure out where golden opportunities may lie.

However, investment trading isn't just about intuition or sniffing out opportunities. In many ways, being a successful trader depends on utilizing available data and analytics in order to make a trade based on solid and relevant information.

So, in order to take advantage of available data and analytics, investors need to become familiar with the statistical tools that are available to them. This information may come from business intelligence information offered by brokerage firms through their accounts. Other sources of information include the mainstream media and dedicated business channels and analysts.

At first sight, the myriad of information available to investors may seem overwhelming. The constant flow of information may cause the novice investor to feel overloaded with data and numbers. Consequently, it is important for investors to have a clear picture of what all of this information means in order to sort through it and use it to their advantage.

We will present a series of statistical tools that are available to investors so that they can make wise investment decisions based on solid empirical data. But, there's no need to worry. We are not going to get into the specifics of how to calculate each one of these statistical tools. We will, however, discuss what they are used for and how we can trip with them so that the next time you see them, you will be able to get the most out of the information presented.

The most important thing to keep in mind is that practice makes perfect. So, the more you brush up on business intelligence information related to the stocks you're interested in dealing, the more you will become familiar with their patterns, trends and overall direction.

Candlestick charting

One of the elements in the job description of an investment trader is learning to read charts. There are several types of charts which investors must become familiar with. For example, statistical data in graphs illustrate the trends and patterns of financial markets. These are presented in just about every report pertaining to stock markets.

In this section, we're going to look at one very specific type of chart which is named the Candlestick Chart.

Candlestick Charts consist of a statistical model that takes into account the link between price and supply and demand. This link is presented in a chart that is comprised of a number of boxes, which resemble candlesticks and represent the trend of the price of an individual stock.

The Candlestick Chart contains four components: the low price, the high price, open price, and the close price. These four elements come together to produce what is known as a Candlestick Chart. This chart represents the price range of a stock with regard to its open and close price for that day.

Regular Candlestick Charts have two types of depictions. One is a black body, and the other is an empty body. A Candlestick Chart with a black body represents a price range whereby the close price was lower than the open price. In theory, this means that the stock lost value throughout the trading day. If the Candlestick body is empty, then that indicates that the close price was higher than the open price. In other words, this means that the stock gains in value throughout the trading day.

The candlesticks themselves can be color-coded in order to determine when the price has gone up, or when the price has gone down. Generally speaking, investors prefer to use red, instead of black, to indicate that the price has done down. Also, some investors prefer to use green in order to indicate that the price has gone up.

Bullish candlesticks

When referring to market trends, investors use the term "bull market" to indicate that the market is strong, and it is gaining in value. As such, bullish candlesticks refers to candlesticks which indicate a positive trend in a market.

In essence, the bullish trend can be observed when buyers outnumber sellers. In that regard, the law of supply and demand will determine that when buyers outnumber sellers, prices will go up based on the scarcity of the good. Buyers will be willing to pay more and more for a scarce good. Unless the good is so abundant that the number of sellers is irrelevant, prices will always go up whenever demand outpaces supply.

It's important to note that rising equity prices are always an indication of a bull market. Therefore, investors can utilize the data provided by the upward trend of candlesticks in order to call the trend bullish.

One other note: an individual stock may be deemed bullish even if the entire market itself is down. When markets are down, that does not necessarily mean that all stocks are down. In fact, some stocks benefit from a bad market. For instance, stocks that have consistently maintained low prices would become attractive to investors due to their lower value. This may prove to pay off when the markets begin to recover.

Bearish candlesticks

The term "bear market" is used when markets are down. As such, a bear market indicates that the overall market trend is downward. This trend is reflected in the price of equities as they are down from their previous highs.

The rule of thumb used to call a bear market consists of a market reduction of at least 20% from its previous high. This implies that a bear market will emerge when the overall trend of a market has been down for at least 20%.

The same principle applies to individual stocks. When a stock price faces a downward trend, its candlesticks will reflect this trend as well. Therefore, bearish candlesticks indicate that the stock is losing value. This trend can occur regardless of the prevailing market conditions. So, even if the stock market is booming, an individual stock may show signs of losing value.

In general terms, an individual stock may become bearish when supply outpaces demand. In this case, there are more sellers than buyers. Consequently, sellers must accept a reduced price in order to sell their equities. The more sellers there are in the market, the more the price will be pushed down.

It's worth noting that when a stock enters the bear market territory, an investor must decide whether it's better to hold on to the stock and wait for a rebound or sell short and cut losses. The most important consideration in this regard is that bearish trends must be taken seriously, and positions must be closed in order to prevent considerable losses.

The ABCD pattern

The ABCD pattern is a statistical model that uses data in order to determine the potential of long positions. In this case, long positions refer to the purchase of the stock whereby the investor will take an equity stake in the stock.

In general, the ABCD pattern utilizes intraday data to measure the trend of the stock. In addition, this model factors in a set risk for the stock in question. It also measures what is known as a breakout level.

In short, the risk level is the set point where the stock will fall below an investor's expectation while the breakout level is the point where the investors' expectations are surpassed.

The ABCD patter consist of four points:

- A: The stock breaks past its initial high and sets what is known as an "intraday high." This is the point that determines the "breakout" level.
- B: The stock then registers a reduction and fall from the breakout level. This is where the stock set what is known as an "intraday low." This low point is what sets the "risk level."
- C: The stock has a quick, but short-lived, rebound and falls back close to risk level.
- D: The stock then takes off again and breaks through the breakout level.

As you can see, the stock shows a pattern whereby there are peaks and troughs in the stock's price curve. This trend will produce a jagged line which is indicative of this pattern. Ultimately, the investor would be able to make a profit when the stock's price reaches the "D" point.

The trend described above corresponds to a bullish pattern. This means that the stock has shown signs of trending upward. However, the ABCD pattern may also show signs of a bearish trend.

In this trend, the ABCD pattern is the opposite of the bullish pattern.

In the bearish pattern, each one of the points indicates turning points in the downward trend in the stock. As such, the bullish pattern indicates the best time to sell whereas the bearish pattern indicates the best point to buy. Consequently, the bearish pattern can be used by watching a stock that you are looking to purchase. When the stock hits point "D," that would be the best time to buy it.

So, in the bullish pattern, A is high, B is low, C is low, and D is high. When the stock hits "D", it's time to sell.

In the bearish pattern, A is low, B is high, C is high, and D is low. When the stock hits "D", it's time to buy.

The ABCD pattern is a staple of short-term traders who are looking at intraday movements of stocks.

Reverse trading

Analysts closely watch reversals in order to determine the point in which a stock's trend will reverse into the opposite direction. For instance, if a stock is trending upward, the reversal will reflect the point in which the stock will begin a downturn. Likewise, when a stock is trending downward, a reversal would indicate the point in which the stock will begin an upward trend.

Traders and analysts keep a close eye on the candlestick movements of a stock in order to detect a potential reversal. Since the candlesticks refer to the range between the lowest and highest prices of a stock through the trading day, a potential reversal may be evident.

When the potential for a reversal is indicated, it may indicate the right time to go long, or short, on a stock. If an investor is holding on to a stock, the may choose to sell at the top, that is, at the highest of the stock's price right before the downward trend is set to begin.

Also, an investor may closely track the downward movement of the stock and buy right at the bottom, that is, the lowest point of the trend right before the stock is set to pick back up. This is a classic example of the buy low, sell high strategy.

When a trader is able to determine potential reversals, they may decide to put in an option and buy or sell, at a specific price point. This would ensure that the trader does not miss each of the points where the reversal might take place.

Moving average trend trading

A moving average is a statistical tool that looks to flatten out fluctuations in a given data set in order to establish the trend of a stock price.

This tool constantly updates a stock's average price by recalculating the stock's average price at consistent points through the trading. In doing so, the statistical model that is generated enables the investor to determine a stock's trend throughout the day, or even longer term such as weeks, months or perhaps years.

The moving average strategy reduces the fluctuations in a given data set. So, if you are tracking the behavior of a stock for the last month, you will be able to see a trendline emerge. This trendline cuts out the fluctuations and leaves a smoother, flatter line which would indicate an upward, downward or sideways trend.

Common longer-term calculations can be expressed in a 50-day, 100-day and 200-day moving average. When longer-term trends emerge, the lower point in the average price of stock is called the "floor", that is, the support for the stock's price, while the highest point in the average is called the "resistance level", that is, the highest point in which the stock is looking to surpass.

Floors and resistance levels often trigger automatic buy and sell orders. These are key psychological milestones which investors use to determine the overall performance of a stock.

Resistance trading

As indicated in the previous section, the highs and lows of the moving average for a stock set what is referred to as the floor and resistance level.

Both floors and resistance levels are psychological barriers which trigger buy and sell orders. In this regard, investors may choose to purchase options on the pre-determined floor or resistance levels. This is why stocks tend to trade in a specified range.

So, when the stock is close to the resistance level, sell orders and triggered which push the price back down. Conversely, when the stock is close to hitting the floor, buy orders are triggered, and the stock price starts to climb back up again.

To break through both the floor and resistance levels, external factors need to influence investors' mindset so that they can decide to pursue trades beyond the floor and resistance level observed in the price of an equity.

Opening range breakout

Range trading is one of the first strategies that novice investors engage in. This is due to the fact that ranges are easy to spot. In this sense, investors can quickly spot when prices fall outside the range as evidenced by recent trends.

Investors can use candlesticks or moving averages in order to determine a stock's trading range. Therefore, traders will react to any situation where the price of a stock falls either below the floor or breaks through the resistance level.

As previously indicated, prices below or above the high-low points will trigger market orders. However, one of the most useful strategies is called the opening range breakout. This strategy consists in acquiring a stock when the opening price falls below the stock's floor.

This type of strategy is a staple of day traders since traders open their positions every day. Often, stocks open at lower-than-usual levels. This would enable a trader to make some considerable gains when the stock rebounds.

In order to set yourself up to an opening range breakout, you must track the trend of a stock right up until the close of the market. That trend will enable you to figure out if the stock will open at a lower point. This is a stock which you could keep a close eye on.

Red to green trading

This strategy is another staple of day traders. As opposed to opening range breakouts, red to green trading is focused on the close of the day.

In essence, this strategy consists in keeping track of a stock which has been negative for the day and then purchasing right at the end of the trading day. This is possible since a stock that starts out in the red and then moves into green throughout the day will get a boost from an influx of traders looking to make a few bucks right at the end of the day.

This strategy is all about timing. So, it's best to set your buy-sell points so you can be sure that you will not miss on the changes in the stock's price. In addition, this strategy will enable you to close out strong at the end of the day and perhaps make some extra bucks that you didn't expect on making.

Data analysis in trading

Data analysis is the core of successful traders. Day traders, in particular, live and die by the numbers. Thus, if a stock's movements are consistent with certain parameters established in your trading strategy, you can decide to buy or sell. That comes with a keen understanding of the data related to that stock.

The good news in all of this is that most data analysis is already done for you. So, you won't need to look at complex data sets and crunch the numbers yourself. In this regard, there are a wealth of sources which you can count on to provide you with reliable data and analysis. Often, your brokerage account will come to access to data and analytics. Consequently, you will have the option to use that information in order to make savvy trade decisions.

Technical analysis in day trading

Much like data analysis, technical analysis plays a key role in trading.

Technical analysis includes any type of analysis which is related to understanding a stock's trend. This implies understanding statistical data on the stock's price. Also, this implies understanding the nature of the company itself along with the broader economic context of the economy.

Technical analysis is all about utilizing statistical models in order to establish a stock's trending behavior in addition to understanding the range in which it is trading. There are several instruments which can be used in order to conduct a technical analysis. These tools will be covered in depth in the next chapter.

Chapter 7 covered a series of strategies which are rooted in technical analysis. Hence, it is vitally important that all traders become familiar with the various statistical models at their disposal. By understanding how these models work, investors can gain a clear understanding of how financial markets work based on the analysis of price ranges.

However, traders also need to gain a broader understanding of the world around them. This broader understanding encompasses other aspects such as politics, macroeconomics, behavioral economics, among other non-statistical factors that may influence investors' attitude at any given point in time.

For instance, political instability and turmoil wreak havoc on investor's minds. As such, investors may be more inclined to play it safe since uncertain conditions are not generally conducive to positive outcomes.

On the other hand, if a country has released positive information on its economy, job growth, and debt levels, then investors will feel more confident in investing and will choose to allocate more resources toward trading. These psychological effects all stem from a technical analysis of a host of variables that come into play within financial markets.

It is highly recommended that investors become as familiar as they can with the technical aspects of the markets they are trading in and becoming keenly aware of each stock traded. This implies additional research. Nevertheless, positive research is never a waste of time.

The bottom line

This expression refers to a company's profitability. As indicated before, a company's financials are essential in determining whether the stock will be sought after or disregarded by investors.

However, the bottom line also applies to investors. The main motivation for investors is making as much money as possible. So, investors need to become aware of the importance that the bottom line has on their decisions. This means that investors are in it to win it. Consequently, decisions should be made on what is best for your financials. This implies taking emotions out of the equation.

Please remember, when investors keep a cool head, they are able to use their better judgment to make solid investment decisions. When their emotions drive investors, they are only setting themselves up for failure.

Chapter 8: Advanced trading strategies

So far, we have discussed everything from market basics to analytics to some of the most battle-tested trading strategies. As such, the information discussed has been intended to get your trading strategy off the ground.

At this point, we have come to discuss advanced strategies that will enable you to get the most out of your trading activity.

In this regard, the strategies discussed in the chapter are "advanced" trading strategies. This means that these strategies are used by seasoned investors who have developed a solid understanding of financial markets, trading, and analysis.

One word of caution: the strategies discussed in this chapter will allow you to get the most out of your efforts but are not recommended for novice investors. It is recommended that you attempt to implement these strategies after you have gotten your feet wet and have a solid understanding of how your investment strategy translates into your investment decisions.

Gap up, inside Bar, breakout strategy

This strategy depends on the analysis of candlesticks. In this case, the "bars" (candlesticks) reflect the trend of a stock's price.

Since each bar is tracking a stock's price range, the initial bar, also referred to as the "mother bar" serves as the reference for future trades. The mother bar set the high and low prices that will determine the action to be taken.

Based on the mother bar, the next price point is called the "inside bar." The inside bar consists of a new bar set within the range of the mother bar. As such, the inside bar is literally "inside" the range of the mother bar. What this strategy enables traders is to set buy and sell points that reflect the range established by the mother bar.

It's important to consider that inside bars are always relative to the mother bar. And since the mother bar is the reflection of a given range within any definite period of time, the mother bar can be calculated at any point during the trading day.

The use of bars within a trading strategy should be encompassed within the market's overall trend. So, inside bars can be used to trade in accordance with the market trend. This is called a "breakout play."

A breakout play is when the inside bars trade within the direction of the market's trend. When the market is trending upward, inside bars will reflect an upward trend in the individual market price range of a stock. This strategy makes sense when the trend is clear, and there is very little volatility in the market.

When markets show considerable signs of fluctuation or volatility, investors may choose to play it more conservatively and focus only on the mother bar – inside bar trade.

In addition, bear in mind that this strategy is based on a gap up. In other words, this is when a stock opens the next day at a higher price than the close price of the previous day. The difference between the final close price and the new, higher opening price is called the gap.

When gaps are larger than expected, investors may choose to hold on to their positions a lot longer than they normally would. In the case of a day trader, this might mean holding on to a stock for the entire trading day.

Gap up, attempt to fill, breakout

Under this scenario, a stock has moved up from the previous day's close. The gap up at the opening of the new trading day is what investors are looking for in order to drive their breakout strategy.

However, when a stock goes from a gap up back to the previous day's closing price, the reduction in price is known as the "gap fill." When the gap is filled, the stock's price is generally reacting to resistance levels.

For instance, a company that reported higher than expected earnings the day before may experience a gap up on the next trading day. But since the stock's price meets a resistance level set by investors, it may "fade" back to its previous high. In this case, the gap has been filled.

When investors attempt to take advantage of the gaps, they are "playing the gap."

There are several ways to play gaps. The most popular play is by shorting stocks. When an investor decides to short a stock, they are looking to play the gap when it is filled.

It is highly recommended that investors take care in watching price behavior when playing the gap before taking a position. Inexperienced investors may choose to take a position right at the opening of the trading day. While there might be a possibility that the stock's price may continue to rise, there is also the possibility that the price of the stock may revert and start filling the gap.

This is where savvy investors can play the gap and put in a position when they feel the stock has come back down to its low point.

The main takeaway of playing the gap is that trades must always be in the direction of the price. So, if the price is trending upward, then that's the way the trade should go. Furthermore, it is highly recommended that investors closely check the stock's movement in order to determine when the gap might start to fill. This type of tracking may require an investor to check in on the price every 10 minutes.

Once the stock has filled the gap, a breakout play may occur when investors' buy positions are triggered, and the stock begins to gain momentum. So, it may very well pay off to place a call option at the beginning of the trading day and set a put option close to the end of the day.

The gap up, afternoon breakout

In this approach, the gap up at the beginning of the trading day is the reflection of the previous day's trend for that stock. When the stock's trend reverts and begins to fill the gap, stop-loss orders may become triggered.

By the time the stock is done filling the gap, most investors who played the gap up may have already gotten rid of their position leaving the stock to trade within its traditional range.

In this regard, investors may choose to keep a close eye on the candles for that stock. If they detect the candles trending back upward, the stock might be poised for an afternoon breakout. Consequently, investors may end up waiting close to the end of the trading day in order to take long positions. This will trigger the afternoon breakout.

It's worth noting that afternoon breakouts generally tend to happen when the cause for the gap up is related to solid fundamentals and not black swans.

For instance, a gap up might be caused by better than expected earnings. This has come to be a welcome news to a firm that had been struggling in recent quarters. So, investors flock to get a piece of the action. The gap up is subsequently caused by irrational behavior on the part of some investors.

When institutional investors begin to liquidate their positions in that stock, the gap will continue to fill. Investors may dismiss the earnings call as a one-off, and the stock looks unlikely to rebound and will continue to trade within its usual range.

Given the same circumstances, a stock might be poised for an afternoon breakout if investors deem the earnings call to be a sign of better things to come. In this case, the gap fill is a logical consequence of the sell orders triggered by the new high point in the stock. If the stock continues trending upward throughout the day, a new floor might be set, and the resistance level has taken higher.

In this example, the stock may very well exhibit and ABCD pattern and break through resistance levels at the end of the trading day. Thus, investors must be wise in setting this buy-sell points effectively in order to avoid being caught unawares.

Fibonacci retracement pattern

This tool is used as a statistical analysis of a stock's price. In short, it is used in an attempt at setting the floor and resistance level of a stock.

The Fibonacci retracement pattern is based on the famous mathematical concept known as the Fibonacci sequence. This sequence is made up of the following in numbers: 0, 1, 1, 2, 3, 5, 8, 13, 21, 34, 55, 89, 144... Basically, the sequence consists in starting with the number 0 and then adding the next number with the previous number in order to generate the next digit. So, 0 is first, and then it is followed by 1. These two numbers are added, 0 + 1, to produce the next digit which is 1. The next digit is 1. So , 1 + 1 = 2, and then 1 + 2 = 3, 3 + 2 = 5 and so on.

As such, the Fibonacci retracement pattern uses the Fibonacci sequence in order to produce the following ratios: 23.6%, 38.2%, 50%, 61.8%, and 100%. The most common ratio is 61.8% as it is the result of dividing one number with its previous number. For example, 21 / 34 = 0.6176 or 61.8%. This ratio holds up with the numbers contained throughout the sequence.

Next, the high and low points of a stock price are taken, and levels are set based on the Fibonacci ratios.

So, the 100% level would be the highest point while 0% would be the absolute lowest level in the price trend of that stock.

Then, lines are drawn to represent the 23.6% level, 38.2% level, 50% level, and 61.8% level. These points can be used to attempt to establish the floor and resistance level of a stock. Of course, it is not foolproof, but the use of this sequence has proven to be useful in identifying general trends.

In addition, for the Fibonacci retracement pattern to be successful, major peaks and troughs need to be used in order for the analysis to bear the desired outcome. Needless to say, this analysis has yielded rather accurate results over the course of its use in stock trading analytics. Investors would do well to become familiar with this sequence so that they can use their better judgment to establish their price points accurately.

Gap down, fill down, inside bar, breakout

Throughout this section, we have discussed the concept of gap up. Now, we will look into the concept of gap down.

Gap down works much the same way as gap up does. The difference lies in that a gap down consists in a situation where a stock's opening price is lower than the previous day's close. As such, the price is down. When the gap begins to fill, the stock's price begins to rise back to its usual trading range. This type of behavior may be the result of an ABCD pattern that extends of two trading days.

The reasons for a gap down are numerous. Let's consider an example:

A company received negative earnings forecast. Analysts are forecasting this company's earnings report to fall under expected levels. As a result, investors began dumping the stock as at the end of the trading day. When the markets opened the next day, the stock got hammered as the previous day's closing price triggered stop-loss positions.

However, investors ultimately consider that these lower than expected earnings are nothing more than a bump in the road. So, they feel confident that even if the company does report lower than expected earnings, it will bounce back in the next quarter.

As such, investors begin tracking the inside bar of this stock and set up their buy options. It is quite probable that this stock has fallen into an ABCD pattern. So, the gap down could well have been point B. Now, the stock is poised for a rebound.

When the rebound comes, the stock is set to break out as the gap begins to fill. Once the stock has closed the gap and it reaches breakout level, a rush of buyers chooses to get back into the stock as they have heard analysts discussing that the lower than expected earnings is nothing more than a minor setback. At this point, the stock had a breakout and is trending higher than before.

The previous example underscores how psychology plays a fundamental role in determining how price points are set and how inexperienced investors will chase the trend. Thus, it is fundamental for investors to keep a cool head even when most folks are rushing back into a stock after it has rebounded.

At this point, we have covered a great deal of information regarding trading strategies. If you are feeling a bit overwhelmed, I don't blame you. I felt the same way when I first started out in trading. There is so much to take in and so much information to digest. This is why I advise you to take things slow.

That is why the strategies outlined in chapter 7 are ideal for investors who are new to the game. The strategies outlined in this chapter are perfect for more experienced investors. When you are able to combine both, you will become a savvy investor who will know how to react at all times. By keeping cool and rooting your investment decisions on technical analysis, you will be able to set yourself up for success and avoid falling into some of the most common pitfalls that new investors fall into. Ultimately, it's up to you to do your homework and make the most of the information available to you.

Chapter 9: Tips for completing a successful trade

Well, we are almost at the finish line for this book. Since you've made it this far, you have already digested a considerable amount of information. You are now ready to begin your trading career. Even if you begin at the shallow end of the market, you will most assuredly have a leg up on scores of traders who don't know any better. In that regard, investors need to continue growing and evolving along with market conditions. This is a constant endeavor that will pay off down the road.

In this chapter, we will go over some final tips and recommendations for you to keep in mind so that you can boost your chances at of making successful trades more often than not. While it is true that you won't win every single trade, you can reduce the likelihood of losing by improving and building on your skills and knowledge.

So, let's jump into the following tips and recommendations for completing a successful trade.

Building up a watch list

This is my first stop.

Building a watch list will help you keep track of stocks which are of particular interest to you. This list should contain stocks which you have been following for a set period of time but are not priced at a point you are comfortable with.

So, building a watch list with these types of stocks will help you visualize the trends in price. By visualizing these trends, you can see in which direction the stock is going. Whether the stock is trending upward or downward, you will be able to understand where it is going and at what price point you would be interested in taking a position.

Also, you can build watch lists according to an industry. For example, you might be interested in following certain tech stocks which appeal to you. You can look at the trends of individual stocks and then compare their patterns. This type of analysis will enable you to realize how well one stock is doing over another.

One other reason for building a watch list may be related to a certain event you are expecting to happen. For instance, you might be anticipating earnings season. Given that earnings season is a significant event, you can set your watch list and track the movement of your preferred stocks right up until their earnings announcements.

The biggest advantage of building a watch list is that this list enables you to narrow your view. This poses a considerable advantage as compared to having a broad view of all stocks. By narrowing your view, you will be able to take advantage of specific opportunities. If you have too broad of a view, then you may miss out on a potentially lucrative trade.

Deciding on the right stocks for you

Deciding on the "right" stock isn't easy.

Often, investors may become focused on a specific stock or industry. When this happens, investors gain special insight into a given industry. This special insight allows investors to act both on intuition and data.

Also, experience is a key element in determining what the best stock would be for you. Through experience, you will develop a knack for a specific type of stock based on industry, turn of business, or even based on the management team running the company.

Deciding on which stocks to buy also depends on understanding the underlying information related to that company. This requires some additional research into an individual company. As I have stated earlier, research is paramount in developing a successful investment strategy. When you understand the company itself, and not just the analytics based on data, you can gain special insight into the direction this company will be taking.

I encourage investors to get to know the people running a company they wish to buy into. Often, companies are successful because they have the right management team at the helm of the company. Other times, once successful companies take a turn for the worse when new management takes over.

Furthermore, understanding a company's financial position will also enable you to gain special insight as to the direction a company is headed. This is especially true when companies run into debt issues. If a company has healthy financials, then you can be sure that their stock price will reflect that fact. On the other hand, a company with shaky financials met exhibits and equally shaky stock price. Investors are always wary of companies whose financials do not reflect sound management and clear direction.

That is why I stress the importance of research whenever the topic of choosing the right stock comes up. Don't be afraid to add several names to your watchlist. Your watchlist will be the perfect place to start picking the right stocks for you.

Putting an entry and exit strategy into place

One of the cardinal rules in investing is knowing when to get out.

Inexperienced investors tend to hold onto stocks a lot longer than they should. Or, they tend to sell sooner than they should. That is why seasoned investors understand the importance of having both an entry and exit strategy. When referring to entry and exit strategies, we're not necessarily talking about leaving investments altogether.

What this strategy refers to is having a clear vision about when you will jump in and when you will push back and call it a day. Perhaps the hardest consideration with regard to having an entry and exit strategy is knowing the right time to buy in. Inexperienced investors generally make the mistake of buying into an asset at the top of its price. When you get into an asset at the top, or close to the top, you are setting yourself up for a massive letdown. When the price of an asset peaks, it has nowhere to go but down.

Earlier in this book, we discussed how important it was to avoid following the crowds. When you see in investors flock toward a specific stock, asset, commodity, or any other financial instruments, you are most likely too late. When investors all jump in at once, they drive up the price of any given asset. This creates a psychological phenomenon whereby prices are artificially inflated due to irrational behavior. Veteran investors will know that when other investors flock toward an investment they own, it's time to sell and get out.

In addition, exit strategies pertain to knowing when to cut your losses. Of course, we don't wish to have losses in any trade. But there is the very real possibility it's you will end up losing from time to time and as such, having an exit strategy can be something as simple as setting a stop-loss point. Or, you can set up a put option at the specific price point. When the equities you hold trigger this option, you will be in a good position to avoid sustaining losses.

One other point: investors keep a cool head at all times and know when the time comes to get out. Rational investors are able to keep their emotions in check and avoid making reckless investment decisions due to their ambition and greed getting out of hand.

Purchasing desired stocks

Consistency is the staple of successful investors. Being consistent enables you to chart a course and follow that path in such a way where you will not deviate from it. Being consistent allows you to develop your own investment style. Moreover, it enables you to specialize in a particular sector or industry. As a matter of fact, specializing in one particular type of financial instrument will help you gain an edge over other investors.

By flip-flopping from one investment to another, or from one industry to another, you are only exposing yourself to unnecessary risk. The risk lies in making ill-advised investment decisions due to ignorance or perhaps a lack of judgment.

So, being consistent will enable you to find the right time to purchase the stocks that you really want to buy into. You will gain insights and understandings that come with experience and in-depth research. Consequently, you will not only get the stocks that you want, but you will also get them at the price you want. One crucial characteristic that you must exhibit in this case is patience. When you are looking to buy into stocks that you truly desire, having a clear entry strategy will enable you to get the stocks that you want at the right price. By succumbing rational behavior, you may end up overpaying for a stock that may leave you with disappointment and potential losses.

Therefore, when you set out to acquire a stock, or equity, that you truly desire, you can build a clear entry and exit strategy around that particular stock. You can begin by setting a price point at which you will buy in. That can become a great start to a successful trade.

Paying attention to the market until the trade is completed

When you set out to make a trade, it's important to keep your eye on the ball at all times. Often, investors may relax a little too much when taking a position in a specific stock. If you happen to take your eyes off the ball, you might miss unexpected events that will cause you to become exposed to risk.

This is why day traders have a leg up another types of investors. Day traders are known for opening and closing their positions on the same day. This strategy enables them to cut out any potential risk that may happen while they are away.

The same principle applies to investors who engage in trades and disregard they're open positions during the trading day. I have underscored the fact that markets are often unpredictable and volatile. As such, anything can happen at any time of the day. By disregarding open positions, or simply relaxing too much, you might miss out on significant developments throughout the trading day. That may also lead to missed opportunities.

Of course, I don't mean that a trader should not even get up to go to the bathroom. What I do mean is that it is important for investors to keep their eyes and ears open at all times while they are engaging in a trading activity. In fact, I would even go as far as advising traders to close their positions before they go out for lunch. Again, markets are unpredictable, and anything can happen.

Also, are you, fine traders, to set up are buy and sell points well in advance so that automatic price points will allow traders to focus more on the action that's happening in front of them and not lose focus unfollowing individual price points.

Once your trade has been completed, and the money is in the bank, you can relax and enjoy life.

Selling stocks when reaching original exit points

When you set up your sell points at the beginning of a trade, you have done so based on the fact that you have decided on a point where you're comfortable with selling. When you reach this point, it's best to go ahead and sell. There is always the temptation to hold onto a stock just a little bit longer in hopes the price will continue to go up. That is how many investors have crippled their profits.

Your goal should be to achieve the points that you have identified at the beginning of the trade. I have always said that it's better to be a day early than the day late. There is always that thought of "what if." For example, "what if I had waited just a little bit longer. Perhaps I could have made some more money on the deal". However, this is a dangerous position to put yourself in. When your stocks have reached the selling point that you have determined it's time to get out.

This is why I keep saying that it's important for investors to keep a cool head. When greed takes over, judgment becomes clouded, and investors tend to hold on to stocks longer than they should. In fact, you should sell at any point you are making money on a stock deal.

If it turns out that you could have made more money on the deal, I would advise you to go back and determine what was it that led you to make the decision to sell too soon. This retrospection will enable you to understand where you could have gone wrong and how to address that in future trades.

Reflecting on trades and extracting lessons learned

One of the best investment strategies that I have heard of is keeping a diary. Investors who keep a diary can keep track of their trades and also keep track of their thoughts as they made those trades. This diary, or journal, then becomes a chronicle of the thought process that you have gone through in order to arrive at the investment decisions that you have made.

If you are wrong and have made mistakes, this journal will enable you to go back and see where you went wrong. This isn't an exercise in dissecting failures. Rather, it is an exercise in improving upon your investment strategies.

When you realize the mistakes you have made, the next step is to figure out the best way to address them, so they don't happen again.

Once again, a journal, or diary, is a great way of chronicling your thought process and how you evaluate stock deals. You can derive a trove of information from the lessons learned that you have distilled from both positive and the negative experiences.

The worst thing that you can do is to continue your trading strategy without properly reflecting on how you can improve it. Constant improvement and evolution are critical factors in becoming the best possible trader you can be.

Some of the best investors in history have learned from their mistakes. In fact, many professional investors appreciate failure insofar as it allows them to keep learning and gaining experience which will lead them down the road to greater success.

So, the next time something goes wrong, don't be afraid to go back to the drawing board and ask yourself what you could have done better.

Researching information for future trades

Research is another one of the aspects that I have highlighted throughout this book.

Research is the lifeline that allows you to uncover potentially hidden gems that lie in financial markets. Furthermore, research will enable you to uncover potentially lucrative opportunities which other investors may have overlooked. As a matter of fact, it's quite easy to overlook potential opportunities when they're buried beneath a seemingly endless stream of data.

Of course, understanding and interpreting data is essentially seeing the forest for the trees. That is why your priority should be to have access to as many sources of information as you can. By having access to multiple sources, you can gain insights that a single source may not be able to provide.

Even if your first stop for information is the data and analytics service that your brokerage account provides, you can always seek out additional sources of information. I have always said that you can never have too much information.

Other times, having access to multiple sources of information allows you to cross reference data. By cross-referencing data, you can make sure that the information you are basing your decisions on has been duly processed and verified. If for some reason things don't go as expected, you can always go back and see where those data sources could have improved the information they provided to you.

Conducting constant research is a proactive attitude that will allow you to visualize where markets are going. Furthermore, on-going research will allow you to place an individual stock in the grander scheme of a market. When you can see how an individual stock plays in relation to an entire market, you can determine if you are getting the most bang for your buck or if you need to stay away from that particular stock.

Automating trade processes

The human brain is an incredible machine. In fact, it is so remarkable that it is capable of processing volumes of information at the same time. However, there is such a thing as overwhelming your brain with data.

Every day, we are constantly bombarded with information from seemingly endless sources. The brain becomes very adept at filtering out information that it does not need. Otherwise, the brain would become impossibly cluttered with useless information.

That being said, online trading platforms enable day traders to automate many of the processes that they engage in on a daily basis. This automation reduces decision fatigue in traders. For example, an investor will choose to set their buy and sell points. Once those points have been set, the investor can relax and focus on the events as they are unfolding. The automated buy and sell points trigger when the parameters are reached. Since this is an automated process, the investor has essentially made up their mind well in advance. If the investor should choose to go back on their decision, it might be too late since the system may not allow them to go back after a specific point.

I have also stated that it is important for investors to keep their eye on the ball. So, automating processes is not about taking your eye off the ball. Rather, automating processes is about reducing unnecessary distractions. Distractions can prove to be costly since they take attention away from things that truly matter. If you can make a decision, then put it behind you, and you will be able to focus on the next milestone ahead of you.

I would encourage you to take a deeper look at how the tools at your disposal can enable you to automate as many processes as possible. This will help free up your mind to focus on research and learning.

Attention is a scarce resource. As such we must learn to focus our attention into the directions that will lead us toward achieving our goals.

Conclusion

Wow! I can't believe this book is already over. It seems like we started the introduction just a few moments ago.

But just because the book is coming to an end, it doesn't mean that your journey as a day trader is too. In fact, it's just getting started.

I am thrilled to see that you have made it this far because it means that you have read through everything this guide has to offer. As such, I feel that you are now ready to begin making your first trades.

Just a couple of final reminders:

- Keep cool. Don't let your emotion get the best of you.
- Stay focused. Don't take your eyes off the ball.
- Take a break. Don't be afraid to unplug when you need to.
- Do your homework. It pays to keep up your research.
- Play it safe. But also play to win.

These reminders are based on what I do myself. I believe in keeping cool even when things are getting pretty hard. Your focus will keep you on the right path. Furthermore, your motivation will gain momentum when you begin to see the fruits of your labor.

Keep in mind that you can do it!

There is nothing holding you back. The biggest obstacles that you will have to overcome are in your mind. But if you truly believe you can make it, you will. It's all a matter of having the will and determination to immerse yourself in the world of day trading. I assure you that when you see the first successful trades pop in your account, you will remember how hard it was for you to get started, but you will also understand how rewarding it can be.

Best of all, you will be well on your way to financial freedom and security. You will soon begin to build the life that you have always wanted. Best of all, it will be all thanks to your own hard work and efforts. You can feel proud of yourself because you set out to do something really hard that very few even try much less become successful.

You have already taken the first step. So now, it's time to roll up your sleeves and get to work!

I hope you have enjoyed this book. I also hope you have found it interesting and informative. So, please don't forget to leave feedback. Other interested readers will greatly appreciate your honest opinion. Also, it will serve to help me continue improving my writing and my delivery of content.

Thanks again and I will see you next time!
Finally, if you found this book useful in any way, a review on Amazon is always appreciated!

CPSIA information can be obtained
at www.ICGtesting.com
Printed in the USA
BVHW041127240221
600994BV00006B/104